THE ACADEMIC ENGLISH MANUAL FOR WRITING

Robin Scarcella
Director – Program in Academic English

University of California Irvine
UCI Program in Academic English

FOUNTAINHEAD
PRESS

Our green initiatives include:

Electronic Products

We deliver products in non-paper form whenever possible. This includes pdf downloadables, flash drives, and CDs.

Electronic Samples

We use Xample, a new electronic sampling system. Instructor samples are sent via a personalized web page that links to pdf downloads.

FSC Certified Printers

All of our printers are certified by the Forest Service Council, which promotes environmentally and socially responsible management of the world's forests. This program allows consumer groups, individual consumers, and businesses to work together hand-in-hand to promote responsible use of the world's forests as a renewable and sustainable resource.

Recycled Paper

Most of our products are printed on a minimum of 30% post-consumer waste recycled paper.

Support of Green Causes

When we do print, we donate a portion of our revenue to green causes. Listed below are a few of the organizations that have received donations from Fountainhead Press. We welcome your feedback and suggestions for contributions, as we are always searching for worthy initiatives.

Rainforest 2 Reef

Environmental Working Group

Some photos/images provided by Regents of the University of California

Cover and text design by Carol A. Hill

Books may be purchased for educational purposes. For information, please call or write:
1-800-586-0330
Fountainhead Press
Southlake, TX 76092
Web site: www.fountainheadpress.com
E-mail: customerservice@fountainheadpress.com

ISBN: 978-1-68036-364-7

Printed in the United States of America

TABLE OF CONTENTS

Acknowledgments

The *Academic English Manual for Writing* is the product of the hard work of administrators, faculty, and staff in the Program of Academic English of the School of Humanities, University of California at Irvine, academic advisors in Humanities and the Division of Undergraduate Education, and staff at the International Center and the Center for Excellence in Writing and Communication, University of California at Irvine. In addition to authoring this book, various individuals gathered information, revised and edited it, and organized submissions. The feedback from instructors and students was instrumental in creating this edition of *The Academic English Manual for Writing*.

Editors

General Editors

Rose Jones
Robin Scarcella
Anna Striedter

Managing and Contributing Previous Editors

Rebecca Beck
Joyce Cain
Susan Earle-Carlin
Kathie Levin
Robin Scarcella
Anna Striedter

Editorial Board

Cassandra Cruz
Benjamin Duncan
Percival Guevarra
Rose Jones
Rica Kaufel
Larisa Karkafi
Sei Lee
Sunny Lee
Karen Lenz
Kerri McCanna
Carey Minnis
Aziz Qureshi

Gina Ruggiero
Christie Sosa
Heather Stern
Robin Stewart
Anna Striedter
Debra Thiercof

Major Contributors

Benjamin Duncan
Anita Fischer
Percival Guevarra
Rose Jones
Hansol Lee
Jerry Lee
Sei Lee
Karen Lenz
Kathie Levin
Jacob Ludwig
Gina Ruggiero
Arnie Seong
Brenna Shephard
Christie Sosa
Paul Spencer
Heather Stern
Robin Stewart
Anna Striedter
Debra Thiercof
Cindy Ting Lin

Cathy Vimuttinan
Mary Ellen Wynn
Omaima Zayed

Art Contributor, Cover Design

Eunice Choi (front cover, Academic English flowchart)

Special Thanks

In addition to the individuals listed, special thanks are due to

Kimberly Ayala
Eunice Choi
Erica Green
Daniel Gross
Holly Hare
Michelle Hu
Jerry Lee
Tina Matuchniak
Carol B. Olson
Bradley Queen
Anna Wimberly
Carol Olson
Bradley Queen
Anna Wimberly

And all the instructors and students whose assistance and insights over the years have contributed so much to the curricular materials, enlivening the process of writing this book and leading to the completion of this edition.

Preface

Dear Academic English 20 Writers:

Welcome to Academic English 20 Writing. In Academic English 20, you will obtain many opportunities to write. You will compose the different types of writing that are valued at UCI. These types include email messages, formal letters, summaries, arguments, and informational writing. You will gain much practice in writing. This will lead to your developing confidence in your ability to complete your UCI writing assignments effectively. You will also be given many opportunities to develop your reading, listening, and speaking skills.

The instructors have developed a unique (one of a kind) curriculum to meet your needs. Among the characteristics that make this curriculum distinct are its theme-based units, interactive activities, and emphasis on reading university-level material critically, discussing academic topics thoughtfully, and writing university-level papers effectively. Language is at the heart of the curriculum, which focuses on the development of vocabulary and grammar as well as rhetoric. (Rhetoric refers to the set of strategies, techniques, or methods used to communicate effectively in both speech and writing.) Students in the Academic English 20 courses learn to integrate, cite, and comment on multiple academic sources.

Approach and Methodology

Because Academic English 20 courses have shared goals, you can expect shared approaches to instruction in the various 20 courses. These approaches include:

- Regular classroom instruction using a variety of modes for learning, including participating in class discussions, conducting Internet research, collaborating in small groups, and providing feedback to classmates during reviews of their writing

- Ample exposure to the types of reading that is required in order to build your language proficiency

- Multiple opportunities to attend to the language features of your reading and to imitate these features in your own writing

- Multiple opportunities to use language from your reading in your speech and writing in a variety of genres (types of text)

- Completion of oral language assignments in a variety of genres

- Frequent periodic review of and commentary on successive drafts of writing assignments by your classmates and instructor

- Regular reflection on writing, reading, and language development

- Instruction shaped to meet the unique and specific needs and interests of students of diverse cultural and linguistic backgrounds

During fall quarter, you will think about your time, how you spend your time, and why you spend your time the way you do. You will make arguments about why you should make time for certain activities. You will read scholarly articles about time and engage in lively discussions with your peers about time and time management. You will write about your best times and your worst times. You will be challenged to look at time differently and in so doing, you will come to recognize how precious time is and want to make every minute of your UCI experience count.

In winter and spring quarters, you will be examining growth mindsets and investigating what it means to find your voice and raise it. Exploring these topics from different perspectives will increase your understanding of them. If you are taking Academic English 20 courses in these two quarters, you will have the opportunity to compete in UCI's Writing Contest, view live performances, participate in Lunar New Year festivities, and read best-selling books, such as *Mindset: The New Psychology of Success* by Stanford professor Carol Dweck, and articles by renowned authors, like economist Paul Krugman.

In order to ensure that you benefit from the Academic English 20 courses, our program instructors have written *The Academic English Manual for Writing*. Royalties (payments to the writers from the publisher) fund Academic English student events and contribute to future editions of *The Academic English Manual for Writing*.

The manual contains useful information pertaining to the program's policies. These policies will tell you exactly what you need to do to succeed in the course and what to do to accelerate your writing development. By reading *The Academic English Manual for Writing* carefully, you will be able to determine precisely where you stand in the class and what you can do to improve your standing. By completing the comprehension questions at the end of the manual, you will gain an understanding of course procedures and policies.

You have done well to be accepted at such a top research institute as UCI, and you will want to continue your success. This means continuing to develop your ability to use language and writing effectively. Our engaging interactive courses will show you how. We hope to give you a wonderful language learning and writing experience.

Best wishes for a successful academic year.

Sincerely,

Robin Scarcella, Director – Program in Academic English

Introduction

The *Academic English Manual for Writing* is designed to make your experience in Academic English writing classes a pleasurable one. It should answer most of your questions pertaining to Academic English 20 courses and serve as a valuable resource.

The Academic English Program offers four different first-year writing courses: 20A, 20B, 20C, and 20D. The goals include helping you communicate in language, preparing you for:

- The lower-division general education courses and discipline-specific courses that you take. Academic English 20 writing courses will help you prepare for lower-division coursework in which you use English for multiple academic purposes, understanding the situational context in which you use it.

- The key social situations in which you find yourself at UCI

- The reading and writing assignments and oral language activities you'll do in later university composition courses. After completing Academic English courses, you should be well prepared for Writing 39A. (The flowchart below will help you understand the Academic English 20 Writing and Writing 39A Course Sequence.)

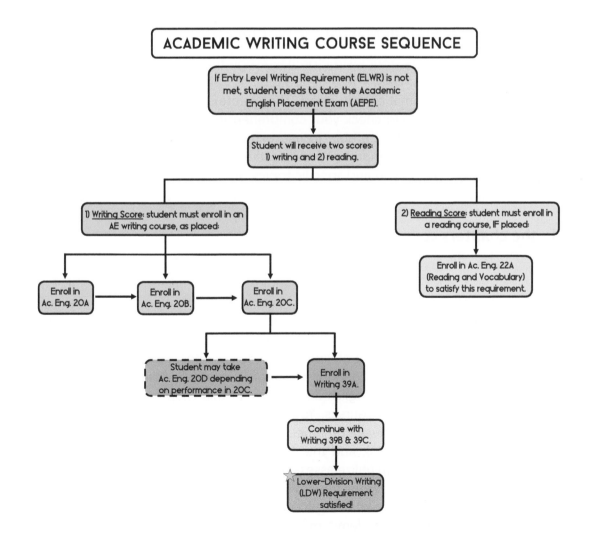

Who is this manual for?

The Manual is for a wide range of students, including students born in the United States, students who have moved to the United States as a child and who have completed many years of education in the United States, and international students coming from many different countries. Those students who are still in the process of learning academic English often find the written demands of their courses very challenging. On top of learning academic English, they need to adopt new conventions of language use, the structure of different types of academic writing, style, referencing, and even layout. All UCI students, especially Academic English ones, need to develop their ability to write well under the pressure of time when taking sit-down writing exams. The specific type of writing they will do depends on the specific course and discipline that they are studying. Students who are majoring in diverse disciplines, like economics, mathematics, engineering, psychology, and film and media studies, have different needs. They are given different reading and writing assignments. Academic English recognizes this variety of needs and provides students with practical skills to help them attain success in their majors at UCI.

Regardless of your academic interests, needs, professional goals, or major, the ability to communicate clearly, using language effectively to meet your own purposes, will be key to your success at UCI.

How is *The Academic English Manual for Writing* organized?

It is divided into seven chapters. Your instructor may assign these chapters as homework, or you can elect to read them on your own. The organization has been made as simple as possible, so that you can quickly find information you need. The chapters contain Insider Tips, Key Points, and student recommendations. To check your comprehension, each chapter ends with reading comprehension questions. You will be able to find extra instructional material pertinent to the chapters and answer keys to the comprehension questions at the program website, http://www. humanities.uci.edu/esl/. To help you find specific topics, you can refer to the index at the end of the manual.

What do the chapters cover?

This section provides an overview to the book. Chapter 1, *Envisioning Success*, explains the program mission and goals and provides you with strategies for obtaining success in Academic English 20 courses. The chapter also describes what you can expect from a Writing 39A course. In Chapter 2, *Meeting Expectations*, you'll learn the advantages of taking Academic English 20 courses, strategies for obtaining success in the course, and your instructors' expectations regarding, for instance, attendance, tardiness, the use of laptops and cell phones, oral participation, feedback, and grades. You'll also learn of your obligations and rights. Chapter 3, *Assessing Progress*, explains the assessments used in Academic English 20 courses. In this chapter, you will learn how you were placed into Academic English courses. You'll learn of the importance of time assessment and strategies that will help you do well on timed writing assignments, portfolios (and their use in Academic English writing courses), and the ways that you are graded in the course. Most importantly, you'll learn how you can utilize assessments to improve your development of English. In Chapter 4, *Supporting Academic Honesty*, you'll learn what academic misconduct is and study UCI's new policies and procedures pertaining to academic misconduct. You'll also learn ways to prevent engaging in incidents of academic misconduct. In Chapter 5, *Managing Your Time at*

UCI, you'll re-evaluate your use of time and learn ways to manage your time at UCI effectively. In Chapter 6, *Using Campus Resources,* you'll learn about the many resources available at UCI to help you obtain new experiences, achieve academic and social experiences, have a healthy lifestyle, and grow as an individual. Chapter 7, *Expanding Opportunities and Choices,* teaches you ways to improve your English proficiency during winter and spring breaks and provides you with practice exams for improving your performance on in-class writing assessments.

CHAPTER ONE

ENVISIONING SUCCESS:
Mission, Goals, and Objectives

The primary mission of the Academic English 20 writing courses is to provide you with the language resources, skills, and abilities to advance to Writing 39 and do well in that class as well as in lower-division university courses. The goals of the Academic English courses are listed below.

Academic English Course Goals

Academic English 20A
Writing effective university-level paragraphs, reflective writing, definitions, extended definitions, a summary, and a short argumentative paper
Developing beginning-level academic vocabulary for writing
Integrating and citing outside sources in paragraphs and short essays
Developing increased command of nouns (including nouns and their modifiers, regular and irregular nouns, articles, demonstrative adjectives, and possessive adjectives) in paragraph and essay writing
Developing a good command of relative clause formation with *which* and *that* and basic subordinate clauses with subordinate conjunctions *because, since, although,* and *but*
Improving on the use of all types of language and rhetorical features related to the use of nouns, verbs, pronoun agreement and reference, prepositions, vocabulary, and punctuation
Actively reading texts to understand, interpret, and evaluate what specific language and rhetorical features communicate
Developing editing skills to reduce errors in Academic English 20A writing

Academic English 20B
Writing effective university-level paragraphs, reflective writing, a summary, and well-structured papers with viable arguments
Developing intermediate-level academic vocabulary and collocations for writing
Developing the ability to integrate, cite, and add commentary when referring to academic sources in major paper assignments, final writing exams, and summary writing
Developing a good command of the use of verbs—specifically verb tense—the literary present, simple present, past tense, present perfect, verb form, modals, passive voice, and subject-verb agreement
Actively reading texts to understand, interpret, and evaluate what specific language and rhetorical features communicate
Developing editing skills to reduce errors in Academic English 20B writing

Academic English 20C
Writing university-level paragraphs, reflective writing, a summary, and source-based academic papers with viable arguments
Developing a high intermediate level of academic vocabulary and collocations for writing
Effectively integrating, citing, and commenting on multiple academic sources in multi-draft writing, summaries, and essay exams
Using cohesive devices effectively to make writing cohere
Developing a range of sophisticated sentence structure and rhetorical features used in academic writing
Actively reading texts to understand, interpret, and evaluate what specific language and rhetorical features communicate
Developing strong editing skills to reduce all types of language errors in Academic English 20C writing

Academic English 20D
Writing university-level paragraphs, reflective writing, summaries, and persuasive academic essays to specific readers
Developing a strong command of academic words and fixed expressions for writing
Integrating, paraphrasing, citing, and commenting on multiple academic sources to support an argument in multi-draft writing, summaries, and essay exams, punctuating quotations accurately
Using cohesive devices effectively to make writing cohere
Actively reading texts to understand, interpret, and evaluate what specific language and rhetorical features communicate
Developing strong editing skills to reduce all types of language errors in Academic English 20D writing

Definition of Goals and Objectives

Goals and objectives are often used interchangeably. **Goals** are more general than objectives. **Objectives** tend to be more specific, concrete, and measurable.

Academic English uses the word *goal* to refer to quarterly aims. You aren't expected to attain each of your course-level goals perfectly, but rather to show that you've reached the goals well enough to compose the kinds of writing that you do for your Academic English course level.

Objectives are concrete attainments that can be achieved by following a certain number of steps or breaking the objectives into manageable parts and accomplishing each part step by step.

In this course, you are in charge of your learning. You have the responsibility and power to plan, monitor, and control much of what you are learning in Academic English 20. The course learning objectives that are listed below will guide you. Your instructor will suggest strategies to help you accomplish your objectives. Try using a combination that works for you in different situations.

> "If you want to live a happy life, tie it to a goal."
>
> – Albert Einstein

 Key Point

*It is not possible for you to attain all objectives with **complete mastery** for all situations. You'll need to figure out the resources you need to gain control of rhetorical and linguistic features and work on improving your control of these features throughout your stay at UCI. By the time you complete your Academic English 20 courses, you should have adequate control of the features you need to complete Academic English 20 assignments successfully. Feel free to discover and use whatever strategies you like to accomplish objectives. It might seem like a lot of work, but if you think about the objectives and focus on just a few at a time—ones that you want to obtain—you can obtain the objectives. Sí se puede. You **can** do it.*

> "How would your life be different if…you had a plan of action towards your goals? Let today be the day…You stop allowing your days to be stolen by busy nothingness and take calculated steps towards your goals."
>
> – Steve Maraboli

Insider Tip

Find the strategies that work best for you and use them to benefit your language learning and writing development. Develop your own wide *repertoire** of strategies for accomplishing your learning objectives. Learn what works best for you.

---

*repertoire
(uncountable noun): the total number of things that someone is able to do

---

*to comprise
(verb): to consist of something, to make up something

---

*blueprint
(countable noun): a plan for achieving something

Key Strategies

- Refer to the objectives throughout the quarter, especially when reflecting on what you have learned and how you can improve.

- Write down the objectives you want to attain. Make the task manageable.

- Track your own progress in obtaining objectives. Use assessment results and your instructors' feedback to check your progress. You can also ask your instructor to check your progress on attaining objectives in office hours.

- Share your targeted objectives with others and get them involved in helping you accomplish them. Talking to peer tutors, writing specialists, and friends about your objectives can potentially increase your focus on them and give you the emotional support you need to attain them.

- Focus on the positive results that you'll get from attaining the objectives—not just passing your writing courses but being able to communicate clearly, accomplishing many of your communicative goals, and enjoying writing.

- Make a plan. Create a timeline for making good progress attaining targeted objectives. You probably won't be able to obtain them perfectly in a single quarter, and many you'll be working on throughout your years at UCI, but you can make excellent progress.

- Take action immediately. Don't wait until the end of the quarter to work on attaining objectives. Taking a single action each day, starting today, will bring you closer to obtaining them.

Academic English Learning Objectives for Writing Coursework (Academic English 20A-D)

You are responsible for your own learning. So you have the responsibility to read the objectives carefully and focus on those that are key to your own improvement in writing and general command of English. You should not accept the objectives uncritically, but instead make decisions about the specific objectives you want to work on. If there are additional ones that you want to achieve, you may want to talk to your instructor. Make a plan to obtain your objectives. Keep in mind that you might think of additional objectives at any time in the quarter. The objectives come from instructor experience working with students like you, but they do not comprise* a blueprint* that represents all you need to know about academic language or writing at UCI.

> "If you don't know where you are going, you'll end up someplace else."
> —Yogi Berra

Objectives

Grammar

Upon exiting the Academic English 20 series, you will demonstrate good control of the following grammatical features in academic writing:

Write down your objectives and track your progress.

- Basic Sentence Structure (subject-verb-object, word order inversion, prevention of sentence fragments and run-on sentence errors)

- Complex Sentences (including relative clauses)

- Verb Tenses (including base forms, infinitives, gerunds, passive structures, irregular verbs)

- Nouns (both regular and irregular, count and non-count)

- Definite and Indefinite Articles

- Subject-Verb Agreement

- Pronouns (reference and agreement)

- Mechanics (spelling, capitalization, punctuation, quotations)

Vocabulary

You will also demonstrate good control of the following aspects of word knowledge:

Insider Tip

Having a strong vocabulary can help you attain success in the Academic English 20 series and prepare you for Writing 39A.

- Word Forms (related parts of speech such as *motivate* and *motivation*)

- Collocations (idioms, fixed expressions, and other words that go together such as *on the one hand, on the other hand, angry with, discriminate against*)

- Transition Words

- Word Choice and Register (including the avoidance of slang in formal writing, the attention to audience, and the feeling or attitude expressed in word choice)

- The The Ways that Words are Used in Grammatically Correct Sentences, Clauses, and Phrases

In Addition

You'll learn to use approximately 50-70 new academic words and expressions each quarter you remain in the Academic English writing series.

Marta Hermosa, a former Academic English 20A student, gives this advice:

"Never give up. You may encounter difficulties in reaching these objectives, but your determination will help you. Focus on making progress attaining a few objectives at a time."

Writing Structure and Rhetorical Features

You'll demonstrate through your writing your knowledge of basic writing structures and rhetorical features. **Writing structures** refer to ways of organizing texts, and **rhetorical features** refer to the characteristics of writing used in special ways to produce particular effects. You'll be able to produce academic writing in which you do the following:

- Structure basic paragraphs (e.g., establishing a unitary purpose for each paragraph and using topic sentences)
- Analyze a writing prompt to identify what the writing prompt asks you to do
- Write effective thesis statements for argumentative texts
- Produce introductory paragraphs for argumentative texts that engage the reader's interest in the topic of your writing, explain the importance of the issue you are writing about, provide relevant context so that the reader will understand this issue (including information concerning the major texts you will be referring to), and introduce the thesis statement
- Use multiple ways of establishing in academic writing (including, e.g., synonyms, alternate word forms of key words, pronouns, transition words, fixed expressions, and demonstrative pronouns) and avoid the overuse and/or inappropriate use of transition words
- Use a variety of ways to add smooth connections between paragraphs
- Support thesis statements and main points with evidence from a variety of sources
- Use quotations and reported speech to support claims, incorporating them appropriately
- Incorporate analyses of evidence to support claims
- Integrate class reading appropriately
- Conclude with suitable final paragraphs (e.g., bringing all parts of writing together and clarifying why the topic should matter to the reader)
- Vary writing appropriately to achieve specific communicative purposes and respond to different audiences and contexts

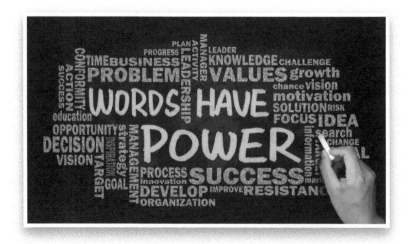

Xilong Li, a former Academic English 20C student, states,

"Stay focused on the positive outcomes you can achieve by making progress towards achieving your objectives."

Types of Writing

You'll also demonstrate the ability to compose different types of writing:

- Reflective writing
- Argumentative writing
- Informational text
- Response to a short story
- Response to scholarly text—article/s, chapter/s, film, lecture, and/or book
- Definition
- Email message
- Summary
- Blended genres that contain a variety of types of writing

Writing Papers with Multiple Drafts

In addition to composing different types of writing, you'll demonstrate the ability to complete papers with multiple drafts by generating, revising, editing, and proofreading. Through carefully structured peer writing reviews, you'll demonstrate the ability to critique your own writing as well as the writing of others.

You will develop strong editing skills to reduce all types of language errors. Each course focuses on reducing particular errors, as indicated below.

- **Academic English 20A:** Errors in nouns, verbs, pronouns, prepositions, agreement and reference issues, vocabulary, and punctuation
- **Academic English 20B:** Errors related to verb tense, verb form, subject-verb agreement, number and articles, as well as errors related to modals, word form, passive, and vocabulary
- **Academic English 20C:** Sentence-level errors related to verb tense, verb form, subject-verb agreement, number and articles, as well as errors related to modals, word form, agreement and reference issues, compound and complex sentences, and vocabulary
- **Academic English 20D:** Errors related to compound and complex sentences, parallel structure, and connecting words, as well as errors related to nouns, verbs, pronouns, agreement and reference issues, prepositions, and punctuation

Julie Karwah, a former Academic English 20C student, explains,

"Once I got into Writing 39A, I continued to make a few mistakes with verb tenses, but mostly I use verb tense correctly now. I'm glad I took the time to figure out how to use verb tense when I was in Academic English courses."

Reading

You'll be able to understand the meaning of challenging academic texts, accurately interpreting the meaning of their key linguistic and rhetorical features.

You'll read actively, using context clues within the text and outside of the text and your own knowledge of language and rhetorical features to take texts apart and understand, interpret, and evaluate what specific language and rhetorical features communicate. You will also learn to annotate your reading.

You'll understand the key meanings of most of the academic words on the Academic Word List.

Seongmin Young, a current 20B student, explains,

"Accept failure as a possible outcome of your effort to achieve objectives. Once I focused on trying to learn a new language feature, I sometimes found I could learn it and use it well in my writing but then later had difficulty using it. If this happens to you, don't be discouraged. Just keep looking at how others use the language feature and keep trying to use it in your writing. It'll take effort on your part, but you'll make progress learning the feature with persistence. Just be patient and don't give up."

Strategies for Achieving Objectives

You may find some of these strategies helpful:

Plan your own learning.

- Create specific, measureable objectives that you can check as "accomplished," or leave unchecked as "not accomplished."
- Set target dates for achieving your objectives.

Manage your learning.

- Use your target dates to distribute the time you will work towards your objectives.
- Work during the times of the day when you are most productive.
- Arrange your environment to facilitate your learning.
- Allow flexibility in your schedule for unplanned activities.
- Seek resources and help when needed.

Monitor your learning.

- Revisit your objectives and make modifications as necessary.
- Reschedule the time and amount of time you will work towards your objectives.
- Use your editing logs, feedback on papers, and conferences with your Academic English 20 instructor and writing specialists from the Writing Center to determine the extent to which you are accomplishing your objectives.

Evaluate your learning.

- Celebrate successes.
- Identify what works well for you and what does not work well.
- Connect with campus resources that can help you achieve your objectives.

Remember:

Learning involves identifying the strategies that work well for you and the strategies that do not work well for you. If you have difficulty achieving your objectives, talk to others to find new strategies to achieve your objectives. Divide your objectives into smaller parts that are easier for you to achieve.

A WORD OF CAUTION

Language development does not proceed in a linear fashion, involving, for instance, the development of first one language feature and then a second and a third, in a smooth, orderly fashion. Rather, language acquisition involves multiple complex processes that are messy and not as orderly as the objectives listed above imply.

Tammy Deng, a former Academic English 20 student, says,

"For a long time, I thought the objectives were useless. Then when I became serious about making progress towards achieving them, I saw immediate results. It was as if a switch was flipped inside of me and my unconscious mind suddenly had a target to go after. My feelings of being overwhelmed flew out the door."

Preparing for Writing 39

Most Academic English 20 students want to know what to expect from Writing 39A. This section provides is some helpful information.

What to Expect from a Writing 39A Class

Academic English students may be under the impression that Writing 39A is a continuation of what they have been doing in Academic English, and that is partially true. What the two programs share includes a deep and detailed commitment to writing pedagogy, including instruction tailored to student need, and substantial, regular feedback on written work. However there are significant differences between the two programs as well. Academic English has a highly regulated, uniform curriculum that uses a point system and includes substantial grammar instruction. Writing 39A uses portfolio assessment, and the course emphasizes rhetoric—including style—genre, and audience awareness. Writing 39A sections also vary in terms of both reading and writing assignments.

Writing 39 instructor Anita Fischer initially wrote this section, with subsequent input from Bobbie Allen, Daniel Gross, Brad Queen, and Robin Scarcella.

Tips for Success in Writing 39A

- Expect to read differently, focusing more on language style and effect rather than content.

- Expect to vary the structure and style of your essays and not to write five-paragraph essays with three points and a repetitive conclusion. Meaningful and complex essays can be structured very differently, and often styled differently.

- Expect that you cannot pass Writing 39A unless you demonstrate an ability to proofread your own writing so there are minimal grammar errors. It is your responsibility to get help with grammar from a Writing Center tutor.

- Expect that you cannot depend on translation apps and software to write in English correctly. The resulting English is usually not passing, and often not even comprehensible. Seek help from your instructor, peers in class, or Writing Center tutors rather than depend on translation software. In 39A you will be working in English as much as possible (reading, note-taking, listening, speaking, brainstorming, peer reviewing, drafting). 39A also requires word processing in English.

- Expect to read aloud in class frequently, and constantly revise, review, and edit your writing in order to pass. You must show your revision work for each essay in order to receive credit. Some 39A instructors administer daily in-class writing exercises.

- Expect to take initiative in 39A. Actively prepare for and engage in discussions and reading as well as writing activities. Ask questions in class if you don't understand. Take chances with your writing to demonstrate that you are willing to grow as a writer.

- Expect that the 39A curriculum sometimes makes assumptions about what all students should already know. If there is anything you don't understand about what is expected of you, ask questions accordingly.

- Expect that you will not pass 39A if your work and participation do not demonstrate that you are ready to move on to 39B, which involves rigorous close reading, rhetorical analysis, and academic writing.

Making Friends

Friendships at UCI help students improve their English proficiency, do well at UCI, lower their levels of stress, adjust to university life, and have an enjoyable college experience.

Below are a few actions you might take to develop friendships.

- Participate in UCI's activities and special events offered by UCI's International Center. If you are an international student, you should note that US-Americans who have traveled or lived abroad often enjoy meeting people from other countries. Activities sponsored by the International Center can help you meet people who have an interest in other cultures.

- Participate in campus clubs that sponsor activities that you enjoy or that you might like to try. Take a dance class, join a poetry club, sing in a choir, or sign up for sailing lessons. You might go alone or invite some friends or acquaintances to join you.

- Go to conversation groups offered by the Counseling Center, the International Center and the Writing Center.

- Ask a classmate or two to concerts, movies, presentations, etc. Even if they can't go, once you have taken the initiative, they are much more likely to be open to going with you the next time you invite them or to even invite you to an event.

- Go to ARC (the Anteater Recreation Center) and, when possible, take a friend or an acquaintance. Students can use UCI's recreation facilities, the Anteater Recreation Center (ARC), and Crawford Pool. All they need to do is present their UCI Student ID card to gain access to the facilities.

- Play sports with friends and acquaintances. Many students in the United States like to play sports as a form of relaxation. They enjoy competing against each other in the spirit of having fun. Find out what sports your new friends and acquaintances like to play and plan ahead. You can also join "intramural sports." These sports are for both males and females. Participation is not required, and individuals do not have to be highly skilled. Intramural activities range from traditional sports such as flag football, basketball, and slow-pitch softball to non-traditional sports such as ultimate frisbee and dodgeball.

- Go out to eat with classmates. Eating together is a great way to get to know your classmates in a relaxed environment. You don't have to go to a good restaurant or eat something special. You don't even have to eat an entire meal. Coffee, tea, or a small snack will do it. The Commons, campus restaurants, and even kitchens in residence halls are excellent places to develop friendships.

- Find a movie, a TV program, or a YouTube video that you enjoy and ask a friend or acquaintance to watch it with you.

- Many US-Americans watch sports events. The Bren Events Center is home to UCI's basketball and volleyball programs. It is fun to go to the Bren Event Center to see the passion expressed and exhibited by fans. You can also watch sports games on television. Watching them with friends provides an excellent opportunity to interact with classmates.

- Take advantage of attending small Academic English and Writing 39 courses and small seminar courses designed for lower-division students. In those classes you will have many opportunities to interact with other students.

- Connect with other students in class. Introduce yourself to them and offer to study or work on a project together. If there are juniors or seniors (upper-division students) in class, ask them if they have any advice that will help you succeed in your first years at UCI. If you are shy about talking to them in person, try sending them an email or social media message. Collaborate on projects and assignments. By working with other students on a project or assignment, you can make friends and complete important work. The collaboration can be as simple as asking a fellow classmate to study with you in person, through email or social media.

The following general tips might also help you:

- Spend time with different groups of students. When you're in a new place for the first time, it can be tempting to cling to classmates who are similar to you. For international students, you'll want to establish a group of international friends as a safety net in your first weeks at UCI. However, international students should also do their best to limit the time spent in groups of all international students, especially those from their home countries. Making an effort to meet and spend time with people who are outside your comfort zones is an outstanding way to make friends with UCI classmates of all walks of life and will enlarge your experience.

- Be aware that differences in expectations pertaining to making and having friends may sometimes be confusing or frustrating, and that misunderstandings or miscommunications may occur.

- Remember to be patient with yourself and others. Try to suspend your judgment of others and don't take friendship matters too personally if you run into difficulties.

- Keep in mind that most US-Americans are generally friendly and open but value their privacy and independence. They might say, "Come over any time." However, that is just what they say to show friendliness, not to initiate a close friendship. They do not mean this expression literally and probably won't like it if you visit them early in the morning. When classmates give you a specific time to meet, you can be sure that their invitation is a true one and not simply a display of friendliness.

- Be aware that comfortable personal physical space for many US-Americans is about 24.5 inches (60 centimeters) on either side and 27.5 inches (70 centimeters) in front. Many US-Americans usually have larger personal space boundaries than people from other cultures. If you notice people backing up while talking to you, don't step towards them, as they most likely believe that you are standing too close to them. Standing too close to them will make them feel uncomfortable.

- Don't worry about your English proficiency; just try to communicate your thoughts clearly. Most people don't "hear" grammar mistakes, and those who are worth knowing will appreciate your efforts to communicate.

- Make an effort to get out and meet new people and make new friends. That's the best way to improve your English and experience UCI. You may have to push yourself beyond the easy and comfortable temptation to just spend your time with others who speak your language or come from your home country. However, remember that your college experience only comes once. Make the most of every day. Be yourself. Laugh, smile, and be happy, and others will want to be around you.

- Finally, relax, have fun, and realize that it takes time to make friends, no matter what country you are from!

Insider Tip

It is not rude for international students to ask questions when they are with a group of US-Americans. US-Americans may talk about movies, movie stars, music, musicians, sports and assume others know the context. Most US-American students are happy to answer friends' questions as these questions indicate genuine interest in topics.

What are considered appropriate topics to talk about with friends or acquaintances can vary somewhat.

Many international students comment that they do not know how to start a conversation with US-Americans because of a lack of shared background. When speaking to someone they do not know well, US-Americans tend to talk about fairly neutral topics. Conversation generally begins with "small talk" about the weather or the immediate situation, like a specific class, professor, party, dorm room, or food. The conversation might continue with questions or comments about common acquaintances, sports, video games, movies, or events. As they get to know others better, US-Americans gradually talk about increasingly personal topics.

Alice Wu, a former Academic English 20 student, states,

"I made many UCI friends, mostly by joining clubs and organizations. It was still a struggle, but I eventually found my place."

Comprehension Questions

1. Which three of the Academic English course goals do you want to obtain this quarter? Why are these goals important?

2. What do you plan to do to obtain these goals?

3. Which of the strategies discussed in this chapter work best for you? Which ones do not work for you?

4. What are "collocations" and why is it so important to learn them?

5. What are "word forms" and why is it so important to learn them?

6. Approximately how many new words should you learn each quarter in your Academic English 20 course? What will you do to learn them?

7. What types of writing are you most interested in learning this quarter?

8. Which strategies for achieving objectives work best for you? Which ones have not worked for you in the past?

9. What can students expect to do in Writing 39A?

10. How can friends help you develop your English? What will you do this quarter to make friends at UCI?

 Focus on the positive results that you'll get from attaining objectives—not just passing your writing courses but being able to communicate, accomplishing many of your communicative goals, using language to explore new ideas and develop new interests, and enjoying writing. "

MEETING EXPECTATIONS

At this point you might be wondering what you can expect from your Academic English 20 course and what your instructor will expect of you in terms of your class preparation, participation, completion of assignments, and adherence to course guidelines. You might also want to know your obligations and rights in Academic English 20.

What Students Tell Their Friends about Academic English 20 Courses

The good news is that you can expect to benefit from them. When asked why they would recommend the course to a friend, this is how former Academic English students replied:

- **You'll improve your knowledge of academic English and writing.** You'll learn the aspects of English vocabulary, grammar, and discourse that characterize academic language as well as ways to adapt your English and writing techniques to diverse university situations. You will learn of the rhetorical and language choices you can make to produce complex, persuasive and sophisticated answers to a broad range of questions.

- **You'll learn to revise and edit your own writing systematically so that your writing contains minimal grammar errors.** You'll discover revision strategies that work for you and are tailored to your learning style.

- **You'll learn to think and write in English without relying on translation apps and software.** By interacting with your instructor, classmates, Writing Center tutors and others in English as much as possible, you will see improvement in your reading, note-taking, listening, speaking, brainstorming, peer-reviewing, and drafting skills. This will make your transition to Writing 39A much smoother.

- **You'll be in a small class and get lots of attention from your instructor.** Your Academic English 20 class has no more than 18 students. You'll get to know your classmates and instructor well and have lots of opportunities to interact with them, receive feedback on your writing, and share your writing accomplishments.

You can take whatever you learn in Academic English 20 courses and transfer it to your major or field, Writing 39, and real world contexts.

- **What you learn will improve your grades in other classes.** You'll take the language and writing abilities and skills that you develop in Academic English 20 with you to other courses, including those in WR 39 and your major.

- **This is a course that will help you not only in Writing 39 but also in other lower-division university courses.** You'll learn useful reading, writing, oral language, and study abilities, skills, and strategies that will help you improve your grades in classes with heavy language demands.

- **You'll have lots of opportunities to practice English.** This is a course that requires lots of practice.

- **You'll learn about language and writing in a whole different way.** You'll learn the importance of thinking about language and writing use in specific situations and ways to vary this use. You'll also develop the ability to come up with original ideas and find evidence to support them. You'll also learn to come up with original ideas, find evidence to support them, and develop your voice.

- **You'll learn how to imitate model texts appropriately to improve your writing and language development.**

- **You'll focus on a theme of interest and "big question" of interest to you throughout the quarter.** All of the readings, writing assignments, and class activities, assessments, and exercises will help you build the resources you need to answer the big question. To help you succeed, you will be given examples of the kinds of writing you are asked to produce.

- **You'll have a great instructor.** Your instructor will help you by providing useful feedback on your writing and timely and constructive advice on your language learning.

What to Expect from an Academic English 20 Writing Course

Academic English courses are not "traditional" English-as-a-Second-Language (ESL) courses and have little resemblance to them. They are much more challenging and enjoyable than those courses. They require that you learn not only language and language-learning strategies, but also rhetorical techniques and strategies for writing in a fast-paced, 10-week quarter.

Preparation for Academic and Professional Writing

Academic English courses prepare you for academic and professional writing in a number of different ways:

Taking Academic English classes gets you ready for the Writing 39 series. You'll become familiar with writing complex thesis statements, analyzing claims, and reflecting on the linguistic and rhetorical features of your own writing and that of published authors. You'll also learn tools like MLA format and plagiarism prevention that will help you in Writing 39A.

Academic English classes equip you to write in a variety of majors. The class readings come from a variety of disciplines, and your academic vocabulary will increase accordingly.

Your knowledge of academic vocabulary, grammar, and conventions will enable you to communicate clearly and professionally in the workplace.

Insider Tip

Most students need to spend two to three hours studying outside of class for every one hour that the class meets.

Taking Responsibility

In Academic English courses you'll take responsibility for what you do and don't do. Your instructors will not constantly remind you to do assignments, hand in work, and read required textbooks. They'll assign much reading that might not even be covered in class. Still, they'll expect you to read it. You'll need to do work on your own with no one standing over you telling you what to do.

This means you'll need to develop time management strategies. You'll need to decide how much time to put into this course. Keep in mind that most students spend at least two to three hours outside of class per every hour in class.

You'll also have to set priorities and balance responsibilities to complete course requirements. You may think that you are such a diligent student and have learned such excellent study skills in high school that you do not need to study much. *In actuality, there is little possibility of that.* Your Academic English class is much more challenging than you realize.

Joy Liu, a former Academic English 20 student, remarks,

"Success in my Academic English 20 courses came from my taking small steps each day to improve my writing. All those small steps had a huge pay off by the end of the quarter."

Reading the Academic English Syllabus, Class Schedule, and Writing Rubrics

Read the syllabus, class schedule, and writing rubrics carefully and refer to them routinely throughout the quarter. These materials tell you exactly what assignments are due, when they are due, and how they will be graded.

Taking Good Notes and Becoming Self-Reliant

Take good notes and talk to your classmates to get information from them that you may have missed. Your instructors expect you to take responsibility for your learning. When you're absent from class because of a documented illness, they'll expect you to take the initiative to find out what you missed from your classmates and make up the work. You can email your instructors if you get stuck or have questions. When instructors hold review and discussion sessions, they'll expect you to participate, coming prepared with questions.

An Interactive and Extended Classroom

- You'll interact with your instructor and classmates and in addition complete much of your work outside of the class.

- In Academic English, you'll be asked to participate in class discussions and question-and-answer reviews as well as in partner activities and group work.

- Academic English 20 classes are workshop style, so you need to come to class prepared, with your assignments completed.

- Your instructor will hold you responsible for your contributions to group work. This means you should not relax and chat in groups but realize that you are asked to solve a problem or answer a question meaningfully under time pressure.

- A shy personality is no excuse for remaining silent in the classroom. In fact, there is no better way to build up your confidence than by participating.

- When you enrolled in this class, you signed up for a one-unit lab course. This means that you have access to the Academic English Resource Center (AERC), which offers grammar and writing workshops.

- At least once a day, you are expected to check your UCI email.

- You are expected to regularly check EEE/Canvas, the online learning management system used in Academic English 20 courses.

- If your instructor sends you PowerPoint presentations and other attachments, spend time on this material. If it reaches you at a bad time, mark the message "Unread" until you have time to engage with the material.

- You are rewarded for being resourceful and scheduling appointments with your instructor and writing specialists. You can also earn credit for attending AERC specialized workshops and the English Development Workshops offered at the International Center.

- You are expected to be punctual and show up for class—even if you have not completed your assignments. Always arrive on time—both to class and to scheduled appointments.

> "Eighty percent of success is showing up."
>
> — Woody Allen

Mark Lu, a former Academic English student, gives this advice:

"What helped me the most in succeeding in my Academic English 20 courses was connecting with classmates. We shared notes and ideas and helped each other keep informed of due dates and understand the requirements of class assignments."

A Professional Writing Instructor

Most of the Academic English instructors have a wealth of experience teaching university students across the world as well as in the United States. They are all dedicated professionals who are committed to helping you learn language and writing.

Your instructors have both the academic training and the college teaching experience necessary to help you reach the next level in writing.

At times your instructors may seem very demanding and critical of your writing, and you may feel frustrated. Keep in mind that they have read thousands of college essays over the years and they are deeply familiar with university expectations. If you meet them outside of class to discuss the specific areas of academic writing that you are struggling with, they will be able to recommend resources for extra practice.

A WORD OF WARNING:

Using translation services or translation apps and software can possibly prevent you from writing well. Much depends on the translation services and apps you are using and your own ability to use them as resources. They can undermine your ability to advance your development of English or prepare you for Writing 39. Your instructors can fairly easily spot papers that have been translated from your first language into English.

Insider Tip

Your participation in group work can help you improve your grade since your participation can lead to participation credit. They can also develop your ability to use language and writing effectively.

What is Expected of You in Oral Participation Activities

Because language and writing involve social interaction, you can expect to participate in a number of oral language building activities. These often involve teacher-student questions and answers, whole-class discussions and debates, pair work activities, group work—including peer reviews of classmates' writing, and oral presentations pertinent to your writing. Although you might not feel like participating in class, push yourself to do so. Remember that your participation could help your classmates, advancing their thinking. It also allows you to practice using language. Participating in class also makes a good impression on your instructor. Your participation may result in your gaining participation credit that could even affect your grade and result in your instructor's writing you a positive letter of support for graduate school. Also, keep in mind that it is always easier to talk in front of your peers once you get used to doing it. If you are nervous about speaking in front of others in English, prepare in advance. Practicing what you might say in front of others alone or with a classmate is a good strategy. Take a deep breath to lower your anxieties and don't be afraid to pause to gain time to gather your thoughts and to emphasize important ideas.

Group Projects

From time to time, your instructor will ask you to complete group projects that support your writing assignments. These projects provide you with excellent opportunities to practice your speaking skills. Keep in mind that within your group, the members are responsible for participating and contributing to group projects more or less equally. All team members make progress learning when one member does not end up doing all the work.

Peer Review

During the quarter, your instructor will ask you to review your classmates' writing in class and possibly on-line. This will give you an opportunity to give and receive feedback on your writing assignments before you submit the final versions. Carefully read and respond to your classmates' writing and offer constructive feedback. Your classmates deserve the best advice you can give them.

Writing Conferences

You're fortunate to have as part of your required work at least two writing conferences with your instructor. You'll conference once with your instructor before the Midterm. Come to this conference prepared to ask your instructor questions about your writing. You will also have an additional conference with your instructor in the last half of the quarter. Instructors will set up conference schedules with you. During a conference on a student writing assignment, your instructors will encourage you to discuss your writing and ask you questions to encourage you to think critically about the language and rhetorical features that you use. They'll often help you work on revising your work by discussing revision strategies and language that should improve your writing. Sometimes they'll diagnose specific problems that you've encountered and suggest valuable resources that you can use to overcome these problems. They may also clarify issues that have confused you. The conference can also be used to discuss the instructor's feedback on your papers. The instructors will help you identify patterns of errors and help you develop editing skills. The writing conferences are also helpful in developing the vocabulary, grammar, and discourse needed to write specific papers.

> *"The right word may be effective, but no word was ever as effective as a rightly timed pause."*
> — Mark Twain

Preparing for a Writing Conference with Your Instructor

If you actively participate in writing conferences with your instructor, you should make steady progress in improving your writing. To prepare for conferences, bring your writing and any other materials that your instructor has requested to the appointment, review your writing as appropriate before going to the conference (make sure to revise and edit first if your instructor has asked you to), and prepare a list of questions that you have about specific writing assignments, the instructors' feedback, and/or your own language concerns. During the conference, take notes on ideas, strategies, and revisions. Before leaving the office, you should have a clear idea of your next steps in completing a writing assignment and understand the resources that are available to help you. Summarize your next steps. You are expected to show up on time for your appointments. If you miss an appointment, do not expect to reschedule it.

Language and Writing Assistance Outside of Class

You'll want to take advantage of the valuable assistance that the campus provides you. (See Chapter 6 for a more comprehensive discussion of campus resources.)

There are several acceptable ways for you to have a one-on-one writing conference outside of class. You can schedule it with your instructor, sign up to see a writing specialist at the Center for Excellence in Writing and Communication, or see a peer tutor (no appointment necessary). If you are invited to join Project Success, count your lucky stars.* You'll be guaranteed three appointments for writing conferences. You can also attend specialized workshops on writing provided by the Program's Academic English Resource Center (AERC).

*Count your lucky stars
(idiom used in informal conversations): realize how lucky you are

There are also unacceptable ways to receive help that can get you in trouble. Getting a roommate to fix your grammar and asking a friend to revise an essay are forms of cheating in language classes. So is buying a paper on the Internet or hiring a paid tutor to write your paper.

A WORD OF WARNING

Your instructor will notice the discrepancy between your in-class and take-home writing if you cheat, and cheaters obviously do not improve their skills, so they will not function well in their academic or professional future. Academic English instructors report academic dishonesty, and a single report can prevent admission to graduate school. Repeated offenses can lead to dismissal from UCI. (*See Chapter 4.*)

The Academic English Resource Center (AERC)

AERC Grammar Workshops

Academic English 20A-D students who fail a grammar quiz with a score below 75% attend a required grammar workshop held by the Academic English Resource Center (AERC) to make up that quiz. Academic English 20 instructors provide further information about these workshops and make-up quizzes in Week 1. (AERC workshops are the Academic English 20 lab component in the class schedule. There are several workshops each week to accommodate students' schedules.)

AERC Specialized Workshops

Specialized workshops on content and cohesion of student writing provide you with an opportunity to study the reading and writing assignments in depth. Any Academic English 20 student can attend, but the workshops are especially designed for students who are struggling with essay structure and content. As an incentive, you can receive credit for the specific workshops you attend.

Questions and Answers about AERC Workshops

1. What is the "lab" I'm signed up for and does it meet weekly?

The AERC Workshops are considered your lab for Academic English 20 courses, although you are not required to attend every week. AERC offers two types of workshops: Grammar and Specialized Writing. You are only required to attend a Grammar Workshop if you do not pass the corresponding quiz in class. If you do not attempt to make up the quiz, you will receive a zero for that quiz.

The Specialized Writing Workshops cover various writing-related topics and you can choose which ones you would like to attend. Your instructor may recommend one to you. You earn credit for attending the Specialized Writing Workshops, but not the Grammar ones.

2. Are there special AERC workshops just for my level (for instance, Academic English 20A)?

Mostly no. Mostly all Academic English 20 students will attend the same workshops. On occasion, AERC will offer special workshops designed for students in specific Academic English 20 course. These are announced in advance.

3. How do I sign up for a workshop?

You must sign up to reserve a seat each week. AERC uses the signupgenius. com website for this purpose. You will need to set up a free account to use the site. Here are the links:

> AERC Grammar Workshop link: http://www.signupgenius.com/ go/70a0a4da8a62caa8-aerc

> AERC Specialized Writing Workshop link: http://www.signupgenius. com/go/70a0a4da8a62caa8-aerc3

4. Do the sign up links for the workshops change every week?

No. The links remain the same all quarter and all year.

5. When is the best time to sign up for the workshop if I want to make sure I get a seat?

Every Friday afternoon around 5 pm the sign up for the following week becomes available. The earlier you sign up, the better your chance of getting a seat.

6. What time should I arrive? What happens if I am late?

You should plan to arrive a few minutes early to ensure that you find the room and get your seat on time. If the workshop is full and you arrive late, your seat may be given away. Whether it is full or not, no students will be able to join the workshop if they are late by 10 minutes or more.

7. What do I need to bring to AERC?

Be sure to bring paper and a pen or pencil. A dark pencil is easiest for taking grammar quizzes. For the Specialized Writing Workshops, we often have special requests for what to bring (like your book, the essay prompt, etc.), so please pay attention to the directions on the website when you sign up.

8. How will my professor know that I attended?

You will receive an attendance slip at each workshop (yellow for Grammar Workshops and purple for Specialized Writing Workshops). You should keep all attendance slips and follow your instructor's directions on whether to put them in your portfolio or turn them in as you attend. You will also sign an attendance sheet. In addition, in the Grammar Workshops, you will take a make-up quiz that will be returned to your instructor within a few days. Your instructor will then show you your quiz results in class soon after.

Insider Tip

There are many Internet sources that give you practice in using particular aspects of academic writing. Some of them offer quizzes with direct feedback. See the Academic English/ ESL Program's website (www. humanities.uci. edu/esl/) for examples.

9. What if the score I get on the AERC grammar quiz is lower than my quiz score in class?

Your instructor will give you the higher score.

10. Is there a quiz in a Specialized Writing Workshop?

No. You will be expected to actively participate in various activities, but there will not be a quiz.

11. Can I attend AERC even if my professor did not send me. For example, if I received a score of 85% but I would like to improve my score and get a 100%, can I go to AERC and retake the quiz?

If your instructor recommends that you attend a Grammar Workshop even if you passed the in-class quiz (for example "AERC Recommended" is circled on your quiz), then you are encouraged to attend. Otherwise, the workshops are primarily reserved for students who did not pass the in-class quizzes.

12. Does it matter if I was sent to a Grammar Workshop but attended a Specialized Writing workshop instead?

Yes. The two types of workshops are completely different and satisfy different course requirements. You must attend a Grammar Workshop if you do not pass a grammar quiz in class or else your quiz grade will remain a zero. Pay close attention to the workshop schedule to be sure you attend during the correct week.

Project Success

Project Success, a collaborative Writing Center-Academic English initiative, is designed for students who are having difficulty passing Academic English 20 coursework. If you are invited to join the initiative, you'll be guaranteed a minimum of three consultations with a Project Success writing specialist or an Academic English lecturer. These consultations will address your individual instructional needs and questions. Academic English instructor Jacob Ludwig coordinates the project. You'll receive encouragement and personal attention. You'll become highly motivated to improve your writing with an extra facilitator on board to check in with you on your progress and development of your writing. In previous years the overwhelming majority of Project Success students who participated in all three tutorial sessions (over 97%) were able to pass the Academic English 20 writing course in which they were enrolled. While there were undoubtedly other contributing factors to students' success in their Academic English 20 courses, attendance in Project Success appears to be a strong factor. The effectiveness of Project Success is largely determined by the extent of students' participation. If you are invited to join Project Success, you'll want to take advantage of this wonderful opportunity and attend all three writing tutorials.

Top Ten Excuses That Won't Work in an Academic English 20 Course

Academic English 20 instructors, and most faculty members across campus, have heard the following excuses and consider them unacceptable.

1. **I overslept and missed the class.** Set your alarm clock. Use a back up alarm clock if you need one. If that doesn't work, ask a reliable friend to call you and talk to you a while until you are fully awake.

2. **My paper is late because my computer died.** You can't always count on technology. Plan for technology not to work when you need it. You can always use a computer in one of UCI's campus computer labs, e.g., at the Gateway Study Center, the Student Center, or the Cross Cultural Center. (See Chapter 6.)

3. **My paper is late because the printer did not work.** Again, don't assume technology is always reliable. Have a plan in place in advance just in case your computer or printer stops functioning. Many printers are available in the drop in UCI's computer labs. You can always find a printer on campus.

4. **My MLA format got screwed up because of my computer. It was the computer's fault, not mine.** It's your responsibility to make sure you hand in a paper that shows you have followed MLA conventions. Even though you may believe your computer was responsible, most UCI instructors will say that it is your responsibility, not your computer's.

5. **I was so sick I could not even email you to tell you I had to miss the class, so you'll need to excuse me.** You may have been sick, but don't expect your instructor to believe you. Many instructors have grown up believing that simply saying something does not make it so. You'll need to provide documentation of your illness. Your Academic English instructors will need to see a doctor's note verifying your sickness.

6. **There was a family emergency (or death in the family) and I had to miss classes.** This too may be true, but once again don't expect your instructor to believe you. You will need to provide documentation of the emergency or death of a close family member. The death of a cousin, aunt, or uncle will not excuse you.

7. **As you can see from this photo, I was in a car accident.** Your instructor won't know that the picture you show him or her is a picture of your car and not that of your friend's. You'll need to provide your instructor with better proof of your accident. They won't excuse minor car accidents that have resulted in little damage.

8. **I was studying for another class. That's why I had to miss my exam.** This excuse is generally not acceptable at UCI. If you use it, don't expect your instructor to give you a make-up exam.

9. **I forgot what time my conference was.** This excuse is not generally acceptable at UCI. If you use it, don't expect your instructor to reschedule the conference for you.

10. **I could not do my homework because I did not have the book.** This excuse is not generally acceptable at UCI. Try to borrow the book from a classmate or friend or tell your instructor privately before the homework is due. Possibly the instructor can loan you a book or advise you.

Academic English 20 Dos and Don'ts

Dos

- **Do** pay attention to your instructor's feedback on your writing. Take whatever suggestions you can. Impress upon your instructor that you value the feedback that you are given.
- **Do** stay engaged during the entire class. Make eye contact with your instructor. Contribute to class discussions. Take notes.
- **Do** turn in assignments on time.
- **Do** stay organized.
- **Do** keep coming to class, even if you become discouraged.

Don'ts

- **Don't** crowd around your instructor before or after class to ask questions. Ask questions during class instead.
- **Don't** be tied to your cell phone or computer.
- **Don't** rely on your instructor to remind you of assignments.
- **Don't** bring your instructor a portfolio filled with disorganized papers and ask your instructor to organize them. Organizing them by yourself is your responsibility.
- **Don't** take up too much of your instructor's time so you prevent your classmates from seeing your instructor or prevent your instructor from completing his or her work. Unless you have an excellent reason for doing so, if you visit your instructor more than four times during the quarter, you probably are taking up too much of your instructor's time. This could possibly give others the impression that you are inconsiderate of your instructor or classmates or are dependent on your instructor for guidance and incapable of revising your own papers by yourself.

Insider Tip

You will do well in your Academic 20 courses if you pay attention to these dos and don'ts.

A WORD OF CAUTION

Late work is generally penalized at UCI.

Student Obligations and Rights

All Academic English 20 students have both obligations and rights. They are described below.

Completion of Work

You are responsible for completing your assignments on time. The program policy is that if you miss 30% or more of the written work for a class, you will not receive credit for that class. Instructors do not accept writing assignments that are turned in more than 24 hours late and they generally penalize late work. Individual instructors may have their own additional policies regarding late and missing work. If they do, they'll describe them in their course syllabi.

The general course assignments are described in your course packet. See the class schedule in the packet. In addition, instructors may assign work in class or via an online platform such as *Canvas*. Students are responsible for following their instructors' directions and keeping up with all assigned work. Students are also responsible for monitoring their progress in the class and carefully reviewing the following section.

Grades

Academic English 20 courses are Pass/No Pass.

The program designed the percentage system to provide equity in grading and lower your anxiety. The percentage shows your instructors your progress in obtaining your learning objectives.

Request conferences with your instructors to discuss your progress early on in the quarter.

Academic English 20A and B: If you are in Academic English 20A or B, you'll receive a grade of Pass and will be eligible to enroll in the next writing level (Academic English 20B or 20C) if you have obtained at least 73%.

Academic English 20C: In Academic English 20C, students who receive a 68% or above receive a Pass in the course. If they receive a percentage of 73% or above, they pass to Writing 39A. If they receive a percentage between 68% and 72%, they pass only to Academic English 20D.

Academic English 20D: If you are in Academic English 20D and you do not have the 73% necessary to pass to Writing 39A, You will receive a non-passing grade (No Pass) and must repeat 20D.

Here is some positive information for you. If you fail an Academic English 20 course, you will likely be able to join Project Success the following quarter. This project will provide you with three free hour-long writing consultations. If you are eligible, you'll receive an invitation by email inviting you to participate.

Absence and Tardiness

Writing courses at UCI are considered workshop-style classes. They depend on in-class collaboration. This makes attendance mandatory. If you have excessive* absences in your class, your instructor has a good reason to fail you. Here is what is meant by excessive: If a class meets three times a week, and you miss more than three class sessions, that is excessive. You should not expect to receive credit for the course. You should expect to receive a grade of No Pass. If a class meets twice a week, and you miss more than two class sessions, that is also excessive. You cannot expect to receive credit for the course, and will instead receive a grade of No Pass.

Instructors at UCI generally establish their own tardiness rules for their students. Academic English instructors consider three tardies equal to one absence and count leaving class early the same as a tardy. Instructors may have additional tardy policy details in the class syllabus.

Use of Laptops and Cell Phones

Laptops and smartphones are welcome in Academic English 20 classrooms, but only when used appropriately for educational purposes and when your instructor asks you to use them. Your instructors want their students to be actively engaged in classroom activities. While you're in Academic English

Insider Tip

Aim to get scores of at least 73% on your Academic English 20 assignments as you progress through the quarter. To help you evaluate your progress, each assignment is given a certain percentage. Details of the assignments and their percentages are listed on the Portfolio Grade Sheet. Monitor the percentages you earn for each assignment. Calculate the percentages you need to reach the minimum to pass the class on an ongoing basis.

*excessive
(adjective): much more than is reasonable or desirable

*grounds for doing something, such as failing a course
(noun clause): a good reason for doing, believing, or saying something.

20 classes, keep your attention on these activities. You should not be texting, playing computer games, doing homework for other classes, or checking email or social media sites. If you do so, your instructor and classmates could consider you rude. The ringer on your cell phone should be silent. Other students should not be able to hear your phone vibrate or beep.

Appropriate use of laptops and smartphones in the classroom can include:

- Reading online class texts or textbooks
- Conducting online research for class activities
- Taking notes
- Writing, revising, and editing drafts
- Completing peer reviews
- Taking pictures of the assignments and notes that the instructor has written on the board.

The university communicates emergency information to students, faculty, and staff. Therefore, at least one person in every room should have the ability to receive Zot alerts.

Key Point:

It is your responsibility to keep track of your own scores each time you receive graded work from your instructor.

Keeping Track of Your Scores

Most students want to have a good idea of how they are doing in their classes. If you are like them, here is some good news. You can track your own progress and know exactly how you are doing in the class at all times. Your instructor may use Canvas, EEE grade book, or Excel to track your grades. Keep in mind that your instructors are not required to track your grades on a weekly basis. It is your responsibility to keep track of your own scores each time you receive graded work from your instructor. This builds your **self-reliance**, that is, your ability to do things by yourself so you do not have to rely on the help or advice of your instructors. As soon as you receive graded papers, quizzes, grammar exercises or other Academic English 20 course work, write down the scores in the Grade Sheet that is in your Academic English 20 packet. You can confirm your scores with your instructor during your instructor's office hours or scheduled conferences.

Progress Reports

You may receive progress reports in your Academic English 20 course during the quarter. The purpose of the reports is to help you identify your strengths and weaknesses in language and writing development. The progress report will also inform you of whether you're at risk of not passing your course. When you are not making steady progress in the course, you can speak to your instructor or a writing specialist to identify your obstacles to success and learn strategies for improving your English.

 If you actively participate in writing conferences with your instructor, you should make steady progress in improving your writing.

Progress Report

This is a report of your strengths and areas in need of improvement.

Your strengths in writing are checked (√) and include:

____ count / noncount nouns	_____ pronoun reference
____ articles	_____ prepositions
____ subject-verb agreement	_____ modal auxiliaries
____ verb forms	_____ parallelism
____ verb tense	_____ vocabulary (word forms, collocations)
____ complex sentences	_____ thesis statement
____ punctuation	_____ quotations
____ other_____	_____ incorporation of evidence

Areas in need of improvement are checked (√) and include:

____ count / noncount nouns	_____ pronoun reference
____ articles	_____ prepositions
____ subject-verb agreement	_____ modal auxiliaries
____ verb forms	_____ parallelism
____ verb tense	_____ vocabulary (word forms, collocations)
____ complex sentences	_____ thesis statement
____ punctuation	_____ quotations
____ other _____	_____ incorporation of evidence

Suggestions:

At this time, you are <u>at risk</u> of failing to pass the Academic English 20 writing course in which you are enrolled. The reasons are indicated below.

_____ You have more than one unexcused absence.

_____ You have missed important class work due to excessive lateness.

_____ You have not done the assignments, or you have done them incompletely or poorly.

_____ You do not take the time to edit your work by yourself.

_____ Your grammar quiz scores are low.

_____ Your midterm grade is below level.

_____ Your editing skills are weak. This might be because you are not aware of the specific types of mistakes that you tend to make, or it might be because you lack knowledge of rules and strategies that would help you correct your mistakes.

_____ Your portfolio is not organized.

_____ You do not make the corrections that your instructor suggests.

_____ You have not attended writing conferences, grammar workshops, or oral communications workshops.

_____ Your scores on sit-down writing exams and in-class short write assignments indicate that your vocabulary proficiency is too low.

_____ Your performance on in-class writing assignments indicates that your grammatical proficiency is too low.

What can you do if you are at risk of not passing an Academic English 20 course?

You can improve your chances of passing the course by doing the following:

- Attending additional conferences with your instructors

- Consulting with writing specialists at the Writing Center

- Scheduling appointments with tutors at the Writing Center

- Completing online quizzes posted at UCI's Program in Academic English website, sent to you via UCI email by the program or your instructor, or posted at EEE/Canvas

- Taking practice writing exams

- Attending class regularly, especially in the final weeks of the course and completing all remaining course assignments the best you can

- Attending additional AERC workshops

- Enrolling in conversation or reading classes (as needed) along with a writing class in the following quarter

Henry Fang

was having difficulty improving his language enough to pass his Academic English 20 course. He received a very low score on his midterm exam and poor scores on his assignments. He struggled to improve his vocabulary and sentence structure. He paid attention to his instructors' feedback and took copious notes on ways to improve his English. In the end, he made great strides improving his English. He passed Academic English 20 and enrolled in Writing 39A. Here's what he advises, "Above all, never give up trying to improve your English. A Chinese idiom says, ' 屡战屡败和屡败屡战的差别.' In English this means that every time you fight, you will find yourself fighting a different battle. Though you will keep losing, despite your losses, you must continue fighting. If after each loss, you reflect on what you have done wrong and take steps to improve, you will win in the end."

What Can You Do if You Fail the Course?

If you fail the course in either fall or winter quarters, you can work on improving your English during winter or summer breaks by completing Academic English Bridge activities.

Feedback Policy

A feedback policy guides instructors in marking compositions. The essay is assigned in three or four drafts, and major drafts, with the exception of a zero draft, are graded. On the first draft, instructors and sometimes peer reviewers comment primarily on ideas and organization. On the subsequent drafts, instructors extend their comments to focus on language difficulties as well as ideas and organization. The grade on the final draft reflects work done on previous drafts; editing and revising are important components of this grade. You will need to submit all drafts of each essay. (See Chapter 3.)

Evaluations of Courses and Instructors

At the end of the quarter, you'll fill out online questionnaires evaluating your courses and instructors. The evaluations are filled out anonymously, and you are asked to take them seriously as they are used to make changes in curriculum, as well as to evaluate the performance of instructors.

Complaints

If you are unhappy with your Academic English 20 instruction or grades, discuss your concerns with your instructors. Schedule an appointment with your instructor to share your concerns pertaining to any aspect of the course. If you are unhappy with your course placements or a particular aspect of the Academic English Program, talk to your instructor or the director. For questions concerning course enrollment difficulties, you should contact the program manager, Eunice Choi at ehchoi@uci.edu.

Enrollment Questions

Below are the questions that many Academic English students have asked in past years.

What do I do if I cannot enroll in an Academic English 20 course that I need to take when my enrollment window opens?

If you are unable to enroll in an Academic English course when your enrollment window opens, please contact Eunice Choi, ehchoi@uci.edu. The program makes every effort to serve continuing Academic English students.

When is the best time to enroll in Academic English 20 courses?

In general, the earlier you are able to enroll in Academic English 20 courses the better. Important: Whenever possible, enroll in Academic English 20 courses before you leave for winter and spring breaks. It may be difficult or impossible for you to enroll in Academic English outside of the United States. Enrolling in classes at the last minute is not a good idea.

What do I do when I believe I should be able to enroll in an Academic English course because I have passed the course, but I am unable to do so?

Before contacting Eunice Choi, ehchoi@uci.edu, try to find out why you cannot enroll in the course. Is it because the course already has 18 students and no additional students are allowed to enroll? To see how many students are allowed to enroll in the course, go to UCI's Schedule of Classes, https://www.reg.uci.edu/perl/WebSoc.

Find the course code, instructor, time and place of the course you want to take. Then, look to the right. "Max" refers to the maximum number of students allowed to enroll in the course at the time, and "Enr" refers to the actual number of students allowed to enroll in the course at the time. Keep in mind that Academic English 20 courses serve up to 18 students.

Insider Tip

Take the progress reports seriously. Don't get discouraged if you are not doing well in the middle of the quarter. Many students make rapid progress after the middle of the quarter. There is still time then to improve your writing and your knowledge of academic language so you can pass to the next level of writing.

What do I do if I need an authorization code to enroll in an Academic English 20 course?

If you are trying to enroll in one of the special tracks of Academic English 20B or 20C for California students, contact Eunice Choi, ehchoi@uci.edu, for an authorization code. If you are trying to enroll in Academic English 22A with an emphasis on either Economics or History, contact the course instructor.

What do I do if I don't like my instructor or I want to move into a different section of Academic English that my friend is taking after the quarter has begun?

Not liking an instructor and wanting to be with a friend are not good reasons for changing enrollments after the beginning of the quarter.

What happens if I cannot take an Academic English 20 course because of a scheduling time conflict? For example, the Academic English 20 course I need to enroll in conflicts with a required course in my major?

See your academic counselor for advice.

Do I have to enroll in Academic English 20 courses every quarter?

If you are a first-year student (a freshman), the answer to this question is "No." You are allowed to stay out one quarter. However, you should see your academic counselor before you decide to do so. While staying out the quarter is permitted, generally, it not a good idea to stay out the quarter, because you may lose progress in developing your English. Sophomores who delay taking an Academic English 20 course even one quarter are at risk of not graduating in a timely manner.

What do I do if I want to enroll in Writing 39A, but I cannot enroll in the course?

Academic English does not authorize students to enroll in Writing 39A. Please do not contact Academic English about enrolling in Writing 39A. Contact the Composition Office. Writing 39A is offered by the Composition Office, not Academic English. The Composition Program authorizes you to enroll in Writing 39A.

What do I do if I am not able to enroll in Writing 39A this year?

If you are unable to enroll in Writing 39A this academic year, keep in mind that you can enroll in an online section of Writing 39A in the summer. Many sections are available then.

My friend told me that according to UCI policy, I must enroll in Writing 39A before the end of my freshman year so that I can complete the Entry-Level Writing Requirement. Is this true?

The policy your friend told you about is only true for students who have not been enrolled in Academic English 20 courses. Students in the Academic English 20 series do not need to complete the Entry-Level Writing Requirement until their 7th quarter.

What if I have finished all of my Academic English 20 coursework and I can't enroll in Writing 39A in 2017 because no course sections are available? What should I do?

Discuss your concern with your academic counselor.

Comprehension Questions

1. What are three or four benefits of attending an Academic English 20 course?

2. What are your responsibilities in an Academic English writing course?

3. What do instructors expect students to do in an interactive classroom?

4. What types of oral activities will you participate in in an Academic English 20 course?

5. There are two types of Academic English Resource Center (AERC) workshops. How can you benefit from each of these workshops (39)?

6. Which of the excuses have worked in an Academic English course? Why?

7. How important is attendance in Academic English courses? Is there a general program policy regarding attendance?

8. When is it appropriate to use laptops and cell phones in class?

9. Identify three areas of English that you are strong in and three areas of English that you need to improve. In doing this task, refer to the Progress Report.

10. How can you use the Progress Report, Canvas, and instructor conferences to build your self-reliance and keep track of your course progress?

> 66 Focus on the positive results that you'll get from attaining objectives—
> not just passing your writing courses but being able to communicate,
> accomplishing many of your communicative goals, using language to explore
> new ideas and develop new interests, and enjoying writing. 99

CHAPTER THREE

ASSESSING PROGRESS

Assessment can be a powerful learning tool that helps you move forward, meet your personal learning goals, and attain your objectives. The results of Academic English assessments, whether formal sit-down exams, quizzes, paper assignments, or informal feedback your instructor gives you in writing conferences, can help you discover what you need to learn or re-learn—and that is good, because sometimes it's best to slow down to address specific weaknesses so you do not fall behind later or hit a plateau in language development.*

*hit a plateau in language development: (verb phrase) to stop developing certain aspects of language.

This chapter explains the Academic English 20 assessment system. You'll learn how you were placed into Academic English coursework, what types of assessments you take in Academic English courses, what kind of strategies can help you do well on timed writing exams, how in-class writing assessment works in Academic English 20, and how you are graded.

You'll make gains in learning English and be more invested in your own learning if you study your assessment results, reflect on the results of the assessments and use them to set new learning goals, and make new learning plans.

The Academic English Placement Exam

When you were identified as possibly benefiting from Academic English coursework, you were notified to take the Academic English Placement Exam, which consists of a reading-vocabulary test and an essay test (see www.testingcenter.uci.edu). The results of these two tests determined whether you needed to take Academic English 20 writing courses and a reading course (Academic English 22A) and which courses to take.

UCI's Academic English Policy requires that you complete Academic English 20 courses before you enroll in the Writing 39 series. Once you test into Academic English courses, you should enroll in them immediately and must take them consecutively until you complete them. If you have not completed your Academic English course requirements by your sixth quarter, you may no longer be eligible to enroll in UCI classes.

John Wu, a former Academic English 20C student, explains,

"After taking Academic English 20 courses, I realized that the assessment supported my learning process and made my language and writing ability stronger. I also realized that I had to be actively involved in my own learning and use the results from assessments to gain better control over specific language features."

The Academic English Diagnostic Exam

On the first day of class, Academic English 20 writing instructors give a diagnostic writing exam to their students in order to identify students' strengths and needs. **In the fall, the Program will not use the diagnostic exams for changing students' course levels or to exempt* students from taking Academic English 20 writing coursework.** If you believe you are in the wrong level, discuss your concern with your instructor. If you are still unhappy, contact the Director, Robin Scarcella, rcscarce@uci.edu. While you will not be given an opportunity to advance to a different course level, your instructor will work hard to ensure that the course meets your particular needs. This year seats in Writing 39 are highly limited. Movement into and out of Academic English 20 courses in Weeks 1-3 is disruptive and causes problems for students, instructors, and academic counselors alike.

Academic English 20 Placement Concerns

Every effort is made to place you in the right Academic English 20 course. If you are an international student, you may feel that you do not need to take Academic English 20 writing courses, especially if you have already completed multiple English admissions tests and have received formal certification of your English proficiency. What you may not understand is that these admissions tests and formal certifications do *not* indicate that you have gained enough English resources to do well in Writing 39A and other UCI coursework. If you are a California student, you may feel that the Academic English course level you have been placed into is not appropriate for you, especially if you were born in the United States or have spent much

*exempt
from + verb + ing (fixed expression): not having to do something. When you are exempt from taking courses, you are not required to take them.

time here. However, you will soon find that Academic English courses benefit you. The ability to write academic texts takes much time to develop and is best acquired in classroom settings where your instructors can teach this ability explicitly, offer you meaningful writing experiences, support your understanding of the style and content of academic texts, and provide you with useful feedback.

You may possibly also believe that you are misplaced because a friend who you believe has your same proficiency level is in a more advanced English writing course. English language development is very complicated and may not always seem fair. English language development is not related to general intelligence. There are a variety of reasons why some students advance quickly in learning English while others do not. When compared to others, some may:

- Be better at processing, remembering and accessing language,
- Have developed better language learning strategies,
- Have a better attitude towards English language learning,
- Have more extensive knowledge of academic English,
- Have more opportunities to interact in English with individuals who are highly proficient in English,
- Have more opportunities to read extensively,
- Have more opportunities to gain experience writing in English, and/or
- Have better writing support.

If you are unhappy with your results, your instructor will counsel you. You will not be able to change writing levels, but your instructor will discuss your placement with you and a plan will be made to help you advance through the Academic English 20 courses as quickly as possible. you will receive counseling and will not be able to change course levels. However, your placement will be discussed with you and a plan will be made to help you advance through the Academic English 20 courses as quickly as possible.

Types of Assessments You Will Take in Academic English Courses

This section presents the various types of assessments used in Academic English courses, describes timed writing, and details strategies for taking timed-writing exams.

To grade you fairly, the Academic English 20 instructors assess your English language and writing development with multiple types of assessments. The instructors will be using these assessments to shape their instruction to your needs and help you achieve the learning goals and objectives outlined in Chapter 1. They will ask you to reflect on course assessments and use them in self-assessments of your progress.

Key Point:
You may think that once you have lived in the United States and attended classes at UCI for a few months that your English will automatically improve. This is not true. Those who take Academic English when required are most likely to develop sophisticated knowledge of English.

The Importance of Self-Assessment

"Self-Assessment is essential for progress as a learner: for understanding of selves as learners, for an increasingly complex understanding of tasks and learning goals, and for strategic knowledge of how to go about improving."

— Source: Sadler, D.R. cited in Brookhart, S.M. "Successful Students' Formative and Summative Uses of Assessment Information." *Assessment in Education.*8.2 (2001): 153-169.

Insider Tip

What's important is that you take responsibility for your own learning. Study all the feedback you receive. You'll want to use that feedback to assess your own progress on a routine basis. That is essential if you want to accelerate your development of English. Know what your strengths and weaknesses are and what you want to learn next.

Quizzes

You'll take six grammar quizzes. They'll give you valuable information about your knowledge of grammar rules and your ability to apply them in editing writing. You'll pass them if you get scores of at least 75%. If you don't pass them, you'll have an opportunity to retake them. The Academic English Resource Center (AERC) will give you grammar workshops and make-up quizzes if you fail any quizzes. The workshops and make-up quizzes are mandatory for students who have failed quizzes. You may also take workshops and make-up quizzes to improve marginal scores on quizzes. Six grammar workshops are provided. In Week 8, AERC gives students a chance to make up one quiz that they have missed or failed. Your instructor will give you information about the AERC grammar workshops and make-up quizzes.

Timed Writing

In addition to the quizzes, you will take several timed writing exams. In **timed writing**, also called writing on demand, you write within time constraints. In most instances, you won't have much time to think much about the topic of the writing assignment or be able to compose multiple drafts. Your first draft will be both your working draft and final draft, so it is important to plan before writing and edit carefully before submitting.

Other Assessed Work

You'll also complete assignments and exercises, major paper assignments, and a formal progress letter, addressed to your instructor. Short writing assignments include summaries, extended definitions, and reflective writing. They encourage you to think critically about texts, synthesize ideas, reinforce new vocabulary and grammatical features, and experiment with the use of language, the organization of distinct genres, and rhetorical features. The major paper assignments include argumentative writing, which is written in multiple drafts. All Academic English 20 students write persuasive essays, and Academic English 20C and 20D students also write a short analysis, responding to one or two short stories or informational texts. In Academic English 20, the instructors refer to this literary analysis as a "Reading Response." Instead of assigning literary analyses, many Academic English 20C/D instructors ask students to imitate a poem, short story, or other type of writing. This type of writing prepares you for Writing 39. In addition to evaluating these writing assignments and exercises, your instructor will evaluate your writing over the course of the quarter, your participation in writing and tutorial sessions, and your class participation.

Throughout the quarter, you'll receive extensive feedback on your writing and language development in Academic English 20 from several different sources. This feedback is a valuable type of assessment of your writing.

Your instructor will give you feedback on how you are using linguistic and rhetorical features and that will help you improve your writing.

Lucy López, a former Academic English 20D student, states,

"When I finally had the courage to reflect honestly on my language use and accept my instructor's feedback, I suddenly began to learn English quickly."

Strategies for Doing Well on Timed Writing Exams

The Importance of Timed Writing Exams

This section explains the importance of timed-writing in Academic English 20 courses and suggests strategies for doing well on these exams.

Writing under the pressure of time is one way to show your comprehension of a subject and your ability to effectively communicate your thoughts. You may take UCI courses that require you to show your knowledge of past lectures and reading assignments in timed writing situations. You'll have to use the right academic tone in these situations. Tone is usually used to refer to the general feeling or attitude expressed by a piece of writing. You'll want to seem academic and objective. On your sit-down exams at UCI, you'll want your instructors to see that you take the task seriously, that you know what you are writing about, and that you can apply what your instructor has taught to convey your ideas with clarity.*

*conveying ideas with clarity
to convey your ideas with clarity (verb phrase): to express your thoughts in a way others understand

There's no way you'll be likely to come up with a great piece of writing that looks as though you carefully wrote it over the course of weeks. Timed writing is a form of assessment you will likely encounter regularly. Formulating effective strategies for writing under the pressure of time could help you succeed in Academic English, in other courses at UCI, and on graduate admissions tests.

Because of the pressure timed writing causes, writing in a timed setting can make even the most confident writers become stumped* and question the effectiveness of their writing. Although timed writing varies in terms of content, purpose, and audience, there are certain strategies that can be used in almost any timed situation to make your writing more productive and meaningful.

* stumped
(adjective—informal): unable to think of language or respond to something (like a test question)

Strategies for Taking Timed Essay Exams

Strategy 1: Plan your approach.

Planning your approach to sit-down writing exams can save you time later and lower your anxieties during the exam. Before you take the exam, even when you are at home, plan your time. Think about how you will organize your time in order to analyze and understand the reading, get your ideas together, and edit your exam.

Strategy 2: Understand the writing prompt.

Key Point:

When deciding how you will respond to a prompt, look for key verbs such as *discuss*, *evaluate*, and *compare*, that give you specific instruction for your writing. It is important that you identify these verbs because they are directives that give you instructions.

One of the first things you will want to do is read and reread the writing prompt. Understanding the writing prompt is one of the most important steps you can take to obtain success on writing assignments and timed exams.

What are writing prompts?

- They are statements and questions that focus on a topic or issue.
- They ask students to respond to questions in writing.
- They are frequently used in university classes.
- They are included on undergraduate and graduate admissions exams.

You will need to know how to **unpack** the writing prompts—that is, take them apart to analyze what they ask you to do. This valuable skill is one of the most useful you will learn.

Asking Questions

Before taking writing exams, try asking yourself these types of questions:

- What is the purpose of the exam?
- What type of writing does the prompt require? Does it require a persuasive argument, an analysis of a narrative, a comparison or something else?
- What information should be included and where should it go?
- Who is the audience and what are the audience's expectations?

In the Academic English 20 courses, most writing prompts ask you to analyze a reading and respond to it. You will need to pay attention to the nouns and verbs in the prompt that tell you what you are supposed to do.

Peter the Anteater and UCI students mix it up Friday night before the slam-dunk contest.

Using a Do/What Chart

A Do/What chart helps you analyze writing prompts. To complete a DO/WHAT chart, underline the verbs that describe what you need to *do* in the prompt. Then construct a DO/WHAT chart. Draw a line down the middle of the page. List the verbs that you have underlined in the left-hand column and explain what the verbs ask you to do in the right-hand column.

Below is a blank do/what chart for you to use when analyzing writing prompts. If you find the chart helpful, you will want to use it when taking Academic English sit-down writing exams.

Do/What Chart

DO	WHAT

Strategy 3: Read the reading passage again and again.

It is important you do not just skim the reading passage of the writing exam looking for keywords, because you may miss essential details and may not fully comprehend the content or overall message. Instead, you should dedicate time to thoroughly consider the reading. Remember that many students get anxious during the exam and read the passage too quickly or overlook important parts of it. Slow yourself down. Take time to read the passage twice, circle, underline, or highlight the important parts, interesting words you could quote, and parts you don't understand. Don't forget to read the footnotes. That's often where you'll find out the source of the reading passage. You'll need the source when you are describing the reading passage. If there is a list of useful words and expressions or grammar tips, you'll want to read them; study the sample sentences; and note any words, expressions, or grammar tips you might want to use in your writing.

Strategy 4: Organize your writing before you start.

You'll have to find your own way of organizing your essay before you start. Most students find that taking some time to brainstorm helps. Even writing a rough outline with just a few key words or phrases can help you to stay on task and keep your argument moving towards its goal. Try making a brief

Key Point:

Being aware of what you do not understand is important. Mark, circle, or highlight the words that you need to understand but don't, and then look them up in a dictionary.

outline, jotting down key words and phrases, or drawing a diagram showing the main ideas you want to cover. You can find an area in the test booklet or writing prompt to write notes or draw the components of your essay. Here are some questions that might help you get your ideas together:

- What is your thesis statement, main point, or argument?
- What is the key point of each body paragraph?
- What order will your body paragraphs go in?

If you make an outline or jot down key words, don't forget to periodically refer back to your outline or notes while writing so that you stay on track. Use each paragraph to state a point and develop the key ideas you have laid out. Having a plan helps to ensure that each paragraph has a clear purpose and intent.

Organizing Tips

A good idea is to include the following components in your timed writing:

- *Introduction*—Briefly summarize the reading by introducing the title of the reading, the author's name, and main point(s). State your thesis, which should respond directly to the writing prompt. The thesis does not have to list all the subtopics or points you will present.

- *Body Paragraphs*—Develop only one main topic per paragraph. Introduce your point for this paragraph in your topic sentence. Reference the reading or quote from the reading when appropriate. Explain the connection between your point and your support for the point, for example, from the reading passage, your observations, or the personal experiences you have described.

Insider Tip

Avoid using the five-paragraph formulaic template, since it is generally considered too basic for UCI writing assignments. Instead of listing subtopics and ideas as you would when writing a five-paragraph essay, relate them to one another to support the main point you are making.

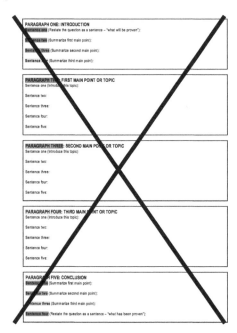

- *Conclusion*—The conclusion can be very brief. Repeating your thesis or summarizing your essay is probably unhelpful. Instead, it is better to leave the reader with a final thought about the topic:

  – What can others learn from this experience or topic?

  – How will it affect you, the reader, or society in general?

  – Why should the reader care about the topic?

  – What are some possible actions or solutions related to the topic?

  – What is the theme or overall message of the passage?

Remember that an essay written under the pressure of time still has to have substance. You have matured as a writer and your writing should reflect that. While you can keep your structure simple for time's sake, do not sacrifice your content. Repeating key vocabulary or ideas is not the same as developing your argument. Focus on explaining the relationship between your thoughts and the support or evidence.

Strategy 5: Edit and edit again...and again.

Remember that no matter how rushed you may feel, you should always take time to carefully edit your essay before submitting it. Instructors tend to be forgiving about minor errors on timed essays, but that still does not mean they will consider a completely unpolished essay acceptable. Look for sentence clarity, cohesion between paragraphs, and major grammar or spelling mistakes. It may also help to read your essay quietly to yourself both forwards and backwards — starting with the last sentence of the last paragraph. It might also help you if you edit for one language feature at a time. If you decide to make some last-minute changes or to correct some mistakes, do so neatly so that your essay's graders can understand your writing.

Insider Tip

While language use and the content of your writing are important in timed writing, the readers will take into consideration that you're under pressure and time constraints. The Academic English 20 instructors who grade the exams won't grade you down if you don't have a title, don't finish your conclusion, don't come up with a brilliant idea, or don't edit your mistakes completely.

Guo Wei, a former Academic English 20D student, advises,

"Don't be like me. I wasted too much time during final exams. I worried about my title, my conclusion, and my ideas. I tried to write long, sophisticated sentences and SAT words. My grades on the exams were really bad. Finally, I realized the graders weren't grading me down for not having a great title, conclusion, and ideas. But they were failing me because they couldn't understand my big words because I couldn't use them right. It took me a while, but I learned that a writing exam requires a different type of writing than a summary, a reflective piece, or an argument."

When you are writing an essay that can be revised, you have more time to experiment with using long, complex sentences. However, in a timed setting, it is best to limit experimentation. Instead, use complex sentences for specific purposes and, when in doubt about how to use them, replace them with simple sentence structures that contain a subject and a predicate (verb phrase).

*convey
(verb): to express, write, or say

Conveying* your ideas clearly is more important than showing off your ability to write lengthy, complex sentences. While you can and should vary your sentence length and structure, use simple sentence structures if you find yourself spending too much time writing a particular sentence.

Li Xia, a former Academic English 20 student, remarks,

"If you are an international student and you are not used to using subject–predicate structures in your academic writing, you'll need to be extra careful when taking sit-down exams. When I first took timed essay exams at UCI, I tended to fall back on what I was most familiar with whenever I felt stressed out. I made a conscious effort to use subject-predicate sentence structures and that helped my writing."

 Key Point

In-class writing exams are important components of your overall course grade. Students receive many points when they do well on these exams and they can use these points to pass the course. The points constitute a significant part of students' total scores. That's why you'll want to do the best you can on these three examinations. They'll help you pass your Academic English 20 course and expand your knowledge of language and the ability to write, giving you practice in balancing a number of cognitive*, linguistic* and rhetorical* constraints*. They'll teach you to adapt what you have learned to a timed writing situation.

In-Class Writing Assessment in Academic English 20 Courses

All writing exams consist of a reading passage followed by a question about the reading.

Examination Scoring Policy for the Final Exam

Two graders read each Final Exam. If the two graders disagree, a third grader reads the exam and determines the score. Exam scores range from 1 to 5. Passing scores on the exam follow:
- For 20A students: 3-
- For 20B students: 4-
- For 20C/D students: 5-

Essay Exam Scoring Policy

Scores are assigned 1 to 5 and may include pluses (+) or minuses (-) to give you a better idea of your writing progress.

*cognitive
(adj.): related to the process of knowing or learning something

*linguistic
(adj.): related to language

*rhetorical
(adj.): related to writing to achieve a specific effect, taking into consideration the writer, reader, text, and context

*constraints
(countable noun): something that limits someone or something, or restricts your ability to do something

1-2 (20A) A paper with a score of 1 or 2 is difficult to understand because of the grammatical errors, especially those related to noun plurals and subject-verb agreement. Some complex sentences might be used, but often incorrectly, although simple sentences generally have correct structures. Vocabulary is limited and sometimes inappropriate

Sample Essay with a Score of 1-2

Older generation often stress the importance and failures for young people taking responsibilities for their own acts. That include burdens for other's expectations toward them or possible mistakes around living circumstances. Regardless of outcomes of those possibilities of one from taking responsibility, young people are actually beginning to get in the habit of forgiving themselves for their wrong-doings or their limits due to lack of trial by pushing them hard to the edge of goals.

Things have been rabidly changing as the years went by, and as people experience new advantages of life through the technology developments. As more people are affected by the kind of surroundings, especially young people, they are forgetting hardships of older people went through, like wars and movements for freedom of expressing their opinions that were disregarded by the certain group of people, which was long and painful to suffer, yet learned the importance of values and experience the growing wisdom of facing and overcome such problems.

I see a lot of times, even myself, that parents are taking responsible for their own child. It is clear that it is not their faults or responsibilities to take care, yet they go after every single wrong-doings that their child have caused, even more some parents are eager to defend their child, thus deny the fact that wrong acts have been caused and it is proper for the young people to take care of them.

Now, it is said to be peaceful days, with technology that has been developed and keep continuing reliable society. However, in fact as carefully look around it can be even more dangerous and getting complex as more people, especially those young people with kind of attitude, live together, associate, and increase the possibilities of causing troubles. As time goes by, the issue has been more stressed and became crucially important—that young people need to have courage to face and overcome possible obstacles, and take full responsibilities for the outcomes.

Now, it is said to be peaceful days, with technology that has been developed and keep continuing reliable society. However, in fact as carefully look around it can be even more dangerous and getting complex as more people, especially those young people with kind of attitude, live together, associate, and increase the possibilities of causing troubles. As time goes by, the issue has been more stressed and became crucially important—that young people need to have courage to face and overcome possible obstacles, and take full responsibilities for the outcomes.

Some of the Problems

- Articles (a, an, the) or plural: older generation, the certain group, disregards, wrong-doings
- Word form: specific believes, taking responsible
- Subject-verb agreement: older generation stress, their child have caused
- Verb tense: things have been rapidly changing as the years went by
- Sentence structure: They are forgetting hardships of older people went through. However, in fact as carefully look around it can be even more dangerous.
- Confusing sentence meaning: Regardless of outcomes of those possibilities of one from taking responsibility, young people are actually beginning to get in the habit of forgiving themselves for their wrong-doings or their limits due to lack of trial by pushing them hard to the edge of goals.
- No real thesis

Some of the Strengths

- Vocabulary: outcome, burdens, expectations, hardships, wisdom, defend, reliable, crucially, obstacles, eager
- Perfect forms: have been rapidly changing, have caused
- Passive voice: are affected, were disregarded, have been caused, is said
- Topic sentences
- Transitional devices: however, as time goes by, yet, now, regardless

Insider Tip

Talk to your classmates and instructor about the editing strategies that they use when taking sit-down writing exams. Keep trying different strategies for editing your timed writing until you find strategies that work for you.

3 (20B) A paper with a 3 is basically understandable but confusing in parts. It is grammatically inconsistent and frequently contains verb form and verb tense errors. It has more complex sentence structure than a 20A paper, though not always correctly used, and only a small amount of sentence variety. There may be some problems with vocabulary, such as word form errors.

Sample Essay with a Score of 3

The top concern that young peoples goes through today is not just drugs, smoke, alcohol, or violence. Yes, these are the concerns that parents and elders who cares about their children mostly talked about. But I think the top concern that young people face this days are media, fame, and getting attention. The problems with young people this days is that they are too caught up with how they might appear to others, such as models and actors, they want to be popular, and have people's attention toward them. Take smoke for an example; from the people I know, who happens to be my close friends started to smoke because they thought it was cool things to do. They've seen their older siblings and movie stars smoke, and they thought they'll look cool just like them. Well. They succeed in getting all the attention from people; parents, teachers, church friends, and me, who oppose smoking. They enjoyed being the ones that people talked about. They giggled and laughed whenever they heard their names mentioned from people's conversation. To be honest, they afraid of being alone. They concerned that they won't be known, that they might be ignored and turned down, afraid to have no friends…too worried about facing loneliness. Instead of taking their life to good, they turned to bad to get attention.

If people were to be kind, and honest, will these kind of thing ever happen? I blame no one for this. I also happened to be the one who wanted fame and attention. Instead of radical things, like smoking and gang violence…I chose to be just nice person. Well. I get people's attention alright, not as much though. But enough to be satisfied, that I know I have friends and people who would treat me the same way; nice. One advice that I can give to other young people who face the same problem is that there's nothing to be afraid of being unpopular. Everyone is somebody and it's better to have less attention for being good than a lot of attention for being bad. Individuality, yes, love yourself and respect yourself as who you are. Blame no one, and nothing, but take it and deal with it with a positive attitude. Face tomorrow with a smile.

Some of the Problems

- Articles (a, an, the) or plural: *this days, one advice, just nice person*
- Subject-verb agreement errors: *people goes, parents and elders who cares*
- Word form: *drugs, smoke, alcohol, or violence*
- Verb tense: *they were concerned they won't be known*
- Sentence structure: *The problems with young people this days is that they are too caught up with how they might appear to others, such as models and actors, they want to be popular, and have people's attention toward them. From the people I know, who happens to be my close friends started to smoke because they thought it was cool things to do.*
- Conditional: *If people were to be kind, and honest, will these kind of thing ever happen?*
- Lack of paragraph structure

Some of the Strengths

- Original content
- Clear opinion
- Non-count nouns: *media, fame, attention, loneliness, violence*
- Compound sentence with comparison: *Everyone is somebody and it's better to have less attention for being good than a lot of attention for being bad.*

Insider Tip

Don't use large words or use lengthy complex sentences unnaturally just to try to impress your readers. Use keywords from the passage if you are comfortable using them and know how to use them. It is better to write with words you are thoroughly familiar with than discipline-specific terms or sophisticated vocabulary that you do not know. Using phrases or vocabulary incorrectly, especially repeatedly, can confuse readers.

  You'll make gains in learning English and be more invested in your own learning if you study your assessment results, reflect on the results of the assessments, and use them to set new learning goals and make new learning plans.

4 (20C/D) A paper with this score is easily understandable throughout. Its grammatical errors occur mostly in more sophisticated structures. On the other hand, there may still be a few scattered verb and noun errors. Sentences tend to show a variety of structures, and there is a fairly consistent ability to write complex structures of different types. Vocabulary is adequate but choices may reflect problems with fixed expressions or shades of meaning.

Sample Essay with a Score of 4

Parent's top concerns for their children are violence on television and crime. I think the top concern facing young people today is their ability to fit in with their environment.

This issue of fitting in with the crowd has effect the society in many ways. There are some who turn to violence for their stability in life and some learn to cope and live with the fact that we all fit in this society some way or another.

I remembered when I was attending Grant Elementary School. In the fourth grade I had a friend named Sandy. She was popular and I was her friend.

We hung out together a lot but I had other friends who wanted to be Sandy's friend too, and that was hard. Because when I hung out with Sandy my other friends hung out without me. In a way I just wanted to fit in and be cool like Sandy and her friends. I felt like I knew the whole fourth grade.

One day while we were walking to pay kickball for physical education, Sandy hit her head on a pole. She was walking backwards and once she turned around, "bang" right on the forehead. Everyone in our class started laughing except for me. Sandy looked like she wanted to cry but didn't dare to. She took a glance at me and ran to the teacher. During the week my social life seem to have gotten quiet. No one really talked to me after that. Not my friends nor Sandy's friends. Later I found out that Sandy spread a rumor about me laughing at her hysterically when she hit the pole. I was crushed for that day on I didn't have anyone.

That's a lesson in all of this. I didn't turn to violence for my problems but I know most of my friends did. The sad part if, is that I watch my peers turn to gangs, drug abuse and even crimes. I've learned at growing up with different kinds of people. The most important part is changing who you are as a person and taking what you want in your life, not what others want. I'm a growing young adult and my advice to all the growing young adults is that, "You the only person who can change anything about yourself." I say that because even is we watch, grow up with despair, listen to others. It's not those things that changes us as an individual it's ourselves.

From all my experiences growing up in America I've learned to be the person I want to be. I've become a stronger individual as well as having a great group of friends. I was always faced by violence but I didn't let it devour me.

Some of the Problems

- Verb form: *the issue of fitting in has effect the society; I've learned at growing up.*

- Verb tense: *I remembered; During the week my social life seem to have gotten quiet.*

- Sentence structure: *Not my friends nor Sandy's friends; I was crushed from that day on I didn't have anyone.*

- Wrong word/preposition: *I've learned at growing up with different kinds of people.*

Some of the Strengths

- Vocabulary: *devour, hysterically, stability, glance, despair*

- Introduction of the topic in paragraph 1

- Sentence complexity and variety: *There some who turn to violence for their stability in life and some learn to cope and live with the fact that we all fit in this society some way or another.*

- Relevant personal example

5 (39A) A paper with this score clearly indicates strong English proficiency. It is easily understandable and fluent. There may be some errors in basic grammar or vocabulary, but they do not interfere with communication.

Sample Essay with a Score of 5

Drugs and alcohol affect many adolescents today. Teenagers have either tried an illegal substance or know someone who has. It is unlikely that you find a high school student who hasn't experienced the consequences of drugs or alcohol, whether it was with family, friends, or themselves.

Everyone is to blame for the downfall of an addicted teenager. Family, the media, society, even movies portray the gruesome images of the effects of abusing drugs and/or alcohol. Drugs can be seen on billboards. Television commercials, and they are the hot topic for magazines targeting young people. No wonder we see the percentage of young people using drugs climb higher and higher every year.

Smoking is an even bigger problem facing teenagers. A friend of mine started smoking at the early age of thirteen. His surroundings may be the cause of initiating this habit, but it has the consequence of developing a lung disease or cancer. My mother also smokes, even since she was my age (eighteen). Quitting to smoke is not an easy thing for her. It isn't for anybody who has a strong addiction.

Every other month or so we hear a tragic story on the evening news about a drunken teenage driver or some teenager in the hospital for a drug overdose. Politicians enforce laws prohibiting underage drinking or smoking, but the numbers of these tragic incidents still prevail. Every year nationwide high school students get to listen to a session concerning drugs and/or alcohol. Their purpose? To convince students not to take drugs. Has their purpose been fulfilled? It depends on the students. They either vow to never take any drug, think "stop now while you can," or continue to do so if they have an addiction. Who do we point the finger at? Parents, peer pressure, and society are all involved. The only thing they can do is to realize the problem and do something to help the problem fade.

About two years ago, I discovered two of my dearest friends were smoking marijuana. At first I was shocked, then angry, and I confronted them about it. With the help of my other friends, we persuaded them to quit and step-by-step, they slowly limited their smoking habits until they were smoke free. Coaxing them was a successful method, but unfortunately it doesn't work for everyone. It may take a tragedy for someone to realize that help is needed.

There is not solid "cure" for drug or alcohol problem, but there are several treatments. You can reject peer pressure or look at the negative consequences of taking those substance. Hopefully, young people can be aware of the problem and choose to stay in a health "drug-free" environment.

Some of the Problems

- The problems are few and minor: *My mother also smokes ever since she was my age* (verb tense); *Quitting to smoke is not an easy thing* (verb form).

Some of the Strengths

- Complex sentences: *It is unlikely that you find a high school student who hasn't experienced the consequences of drugs or alcohol, whether it was with family, friends, or themselves.*

- Vocabulary: *Coaxing them was a successful method, but unfortunately it doesn't work for everyone.*

- Verb forms and tenses: *It may take a tragedy for someone to realize that help is needed.*

- Supporting details

Juan Pablo Hermoso, a former Academic English 20 student, warns,

"If you want to do well on your sit down writing exams for Academic English 20 courses, sleep the night before you take the test. Once I didn't sleep before an exam, and I was completely brain dead the next day. I failed the exam."

Organization of Writing in a Writing Portfolio

You should keep all of your writing, including assigned drafts of papers in a "portfolio." Your instructor will determine whether you should keep your work electronically or in a binder (a print version). Many students find it helpful to label electronic files carefully and organize and save them on a flash drive or place them in a Google Drive folder. Some instructors will require that you organize your files in this way. These files constitute an electronic portfolio. Hard copies of your work should be organized in a binder or in the way your instructor tells you.

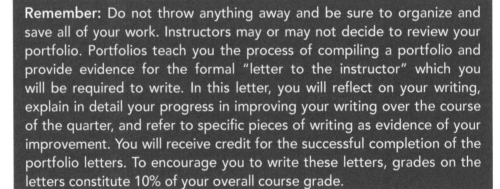

Remember: Do not throw anything away and be sure to organize and save all of your work. Instructors may or may not decide to review your portfolio. Portfolios teach you the process of compiling a portfolio and provide evidence for the formal "letter to the instructor" which you will be required to write. In this letter, you will reflect on your writing, explain in detail your progress in improving your writing over the course of the quarter, and refer to specific pieces of writing as evidence of your improvement. You will receive credit for the successful completion of the portfolio letters. To encourage you to write these letters, grades on the letters constitute 10% of your overall course grade.

Insider Tip

Include all significantly revised drafts—even the ones your instructor may never have seen. This will show the portfolio readers how diligent you are.

A writing portfolio serves many purposes. It can assess your ability to write, enable you to see your language and writing progress over time, and showcase your work. This form of assessment takes into account the processes involved in your writing and the different types of writing you have written.

Designers, artists, and architects use portfolios to give potential employers an idea of their abilities and creativity. Portfolios should show the viewer not only what an individual has achieved, but also what is possible. They reflect your personal style and your abilities as well as your effort to find your own voice and vary your writing appropriately. Photographers seeking work put together a portfolio that demonstrates both breadth and depth. Their portfolios include different types of settings, poses, lighting, background, and subjects. Similarly, students seeking to excel in Academic English 20 can put together portfolios that show breadth and depth, with writing reflecting different types of writings or genres, topics, messages, and ways of expressing attitudes and views.

You should make yourself aware of the expectations and requirements of the portfolio even if you do not assemble it until much later and even if your instructor does not collect it. Basically, when you are completing your writing assignments, each draft has the potential of being part of your final portfolio, so give each your best effort. You'll include your zero drafts, the preliminary drafts you wrote when you were just getting your ideas together. You'll also include all significantly revised* drafts, notes, annotations, class work, and any other supplemental assignments related to your writing. There are no restrictions on how often you can revise your papers in Academic English 20 courses, though only specific drafts are graded. This means that you are responsible for determining how much work you will put into writing drafts and how many drafts you will actually produce. You should include all that you have significantly revised.

Working drafts should reflect what you have learned and how you are able to handle the varying challenges in the different stages of writing. This does not mean that each draft or piece of writing that has been graded should be excellent. Your portfolio should reflect your challenges writing papers. It should show that you were actively engaged in the writing process and thought about your writing carefully, trying again and again to improve it and not hesitating to throw out major parts of your writing or start over when necessary. It should show that you were capable of seeking and using feedback to improve your writing, that you reflected on your language and writing development, and that you were an active participant in your own learning.

*to significantly revise something *(verb phrase): to make major and important changes to something*

Assembling a Portfolio — Record Keeping

Part of good record keeping also involves creating a filing and naming system for your work. You should create separate folders for each course and name the documents in a way that reflects the assignment and the version, so you can easily distinguish different versions. You are responsible for submitting the correct writing draft by the assignment due date, whether your course is online or on campus. Establishing good record keeping habits will not only save you from the stress of having turned in the wrong assignment, but it will also prepare you for the future when you may need to present a sample of your writing to a potential employer or scholarship committee. Saving and accurately organizing your work as you write it makes putting together a portfolio that much easier.

Assembling a Portfolio — Format and Presentation

Portfolios can be put together in a number of ways depending on what you want to highlight or showcase. Generally, your writing portfolio will include the various types of writing that you have written over the quarter. A physical portfolio will require that your writing drafts be printed, hole-punched, and organized—placed into sections by topic, and arranged chronologically. You will place them in a binder or folder. If your instructor asks you to submit your entire portfolio, you will want to make sure that you adhere strictly to whatever guidelines your instructor gives you regarding labeling, organization, and presentation, because your instructor will want to focus on your work and not be distracted by a lack of organization.

An electronic version of a portfolio should be organized and formatted with the same attention and care as a printed version. Instead of a binder or folder, you'll use web pages to display your working and final drafts. Ask questions and follow your instructor's guidance regarding visuals and formatting concerns. Organize your writing by type and then by drafts. Create the appropriate section titles and upload and arrange documents as necessary. Having an accurate file naming system will help you to easily retrieve and upload files as necessary into your electronic portfolio. You may submit your final electronic portfolio in several ways, such as by sending a link or a zip file. You'll need to ask questions and follow your instructor's guidelines.

In your portfolio progress letter, you'll have an opportunity to explain your work and what you've learned. You can direct your readers' attention to your challenges and the improvements that you've made, your developing ability to pinpoint your own strengths and weaknesses, your accomplishment of course learning objectives, and your growing control of language and ability to compose a variety of texts for varying purposes.

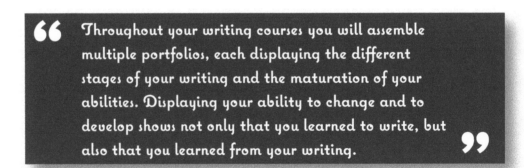

> " Throughout your writing courses you will assemble multiple portfolios, each displaying the different stages of your writing and the maturation of your abilities. Displaying your ability to change and to develop shows not only that you learned to write, but also that you learned from your writing. "

Progress Letter — Putting your best foot forward

The progress letter contains the following:

- An introduction that states whether or not you believe you have obtained the Academic English 20 goals and learning objectives required to move up to the next level of writing, either an Academic English 20 or Writing

39 course (The goals and objectives are described in Chapter 1. Your progress letter should show that you have obtained enough mastery of these standards and learning objectives to advance to the next level.)

- A discussion about your overall progress in academic writing, including examples of areas in which you have improved and the areas you still need to work on (based on the writing sections of your portfolio)

- A statement or two about your editing logs, including how they show your progress in grammar and punctuation, as well as the issues you still need to work on

- A statement or two about the feedback you received on your writing from your instructor and your classmates, including at least two comments you received in feedback that helped you to improve your writing

- A brief discussion of the role that drafting, revising, and editing have played in your development as a writer

- A concluding paragraph that sums up how your portfolio reflects your progress as a writer over the quarter

Strategies for Assembling a Great Portfolio

- Keep copies of all of your work, both electronic and printed. Save all work and save it again.

- Save drafts that contain written feedback from your instructor, both electronic and printed.

- Name your writing assignments systematically to reflect the course, writing prompt, and version.

- Be aware of assembly guidelines: type of work to include, labels, organization format, and presentation requirements.

- Edit your work thoroughly; you'll want to label draft headings and sections. Details count and impress portfolio reviewers.

- Your progress letter should be polished and reflect the best of your writing abilities.

- If you have questions, ask your classmates and instructor and refer to course materials.

Ramon Padillo, a former Academic English 20 student, gives this advice:

"The best advice I can give is this—save all your writing and save it again. I found it easiest to email my various drafts to myself. I also created a cloud space with Google Drive and used Turnitin.com to store drafts."

Formatting

Format

Your progress letter should follow business letter format with one-inch margins. The layout should be block formatted. Do not indent paragraphs. For a model, please see below.

Progress Letter

Peter Anteater
A: Irvine, CA 92697 Telephone: 949-100-800
E: panteater@uci.edu

May 25, 2016

Instructor's Name
Lecturer
University of California, Irvine
315 Humanities Hall
Irvine, CA 92697

Dear (Instructor's name),

No need to introduce yourself here (I know you already). In your opening paragraph, consider taking the opportunity here to discuss how the quarter went for you. More or less challenging than you anticipated? How so? Also take the opportunity here to discuss what is in your portfolio and perhaps the key pieces, readings, homework, or class activities that informed and/or advanced your writing in some way. End this paragraph describing in what ways you grew as a writer. In other words, what did you learn?

Take the opportunity here to get specific. You made a claim earlier about what you learned, right? So take the time here to prove it. What assignments were particularly helpful? What did you learn how to do better? Perhaps you learned the importance of integrating sources. Okay, great. Tell me more. What about integrating sources did you learn? That it's important to provide evidence...? Or how to correctly format quotes and citations? In other words, don't simply state that you learned how to do something. Explain why it was important that you learned this and how you are going to apply what you have learned in future assignments.

Here's another opportunity for you to be specific. Remember, you have a lot of choices here regarding what to discuss: how your writing process has changed/improved, the significance of another assignment, how the reading improved your writing, what you learned from peer-review, etc. Now, obviously, you don't have the space nor the time to talk about every aspect of this class, so choose carefully. Also, remember, if you are going to make a claim about how your writing has improved, make sure you can cite and/or refer to the specific assignment, activity, and/or lesson. If your editing skills improved in Paper 2, then you should be able to provide evidence, for example, "Compared to my editing log for Paper 1, you can see that by changing the way I edited (looking for specific errors instead of looking for all errors), I made great improvements in identifying for errors in Paper 2 and correcting them.

Here's where you can further emphasize the progress you've made in this class, i.e., in what ways you're writing in your portfolio demonstrates how you have completed this course a stronger writer. Normally, this is where you'd thank your reader (me, in this case) for taking the time to consider you for this position (in this case, not a position, but rather to consider passing you). Perhaps you hope I enjoy reading your portfolio. As your final statement, do your best to make a powerful, memorable statement about your writing.

Sincerely,

Peter Anteater

How You are Graded in Academic English 20 Courses

Course Grades

You will receive a grade of Pass or No Pass in your Academic English 20 course. Instructors use a percentage system when grading your work. Assignments and additional work add up to 100%. Your instructor won't necessarily be able to calculate how you are doing in your course on a given day on the spot. That is why you will be asked to keep track of your own overall grade in the course as you complete assignments. Use the Academic English Student Grade Sheet that the Program in Academic English 20 provides. The Student Grade Sheet lists the course writing assignments, examinations and quizzes. It tells you what percentage your assignments are worth. In all Academic English courses **except for Academic English 20C,** 73% is the percentage that is required to pass the course. In Academic English 20C, students who receive a 68% or above receive a Pass in the course. If they receive a percentage of 73% or above, they pass to Writing 39A. If they receive a percentage between 68% and 72%, they pass only to Academic English 20D. If they receive 67% or below, they receive a No Pass. If you receive a grade of No Pass, you need to repeat the course level. Instructors review details about overall course grade, and important related information in class.

Instructors will review your progress throughout the quarter, and they will evaluate you on your strengths and weaknesses. You are responsible for ongoing monitoring of your scores.

Course Grades of "Pass" (P)

A grade of "passing" quality indicates that you did what the assignments asked at a level that ranges from average to excellent. It also indicates that you were able to make good progress in achieving the course's learning goals and objectives (see Chapter 1).

Course Grades of "No Pass" (NP)

A grade of "no passing" quality indicates that you did what the assignments asked at a low level of quality, and you did not achieve enough of the course objectives to pass to the next level of writing. It may be that you often did not revise or edit your work carefully, that you did not take advantage of the tutorial services offered to you, and that your study skills need to be improved. You may have missed too many classes to improve your writing or you may not have completed enough assignments. If you feel you put in your best effort and still received a grade of NP, see your instructor immediately. If you are a sophomore or junior, contact the director to develop a plan to accelerate your completion of Academic English coursework.

Grades of Incomplete

A grade of incomplete is given to students only when their work is of good quality but is incomplete for good cause, such as a serious documented illness. If you receive a grade of Incomplete, you must make arrangements with your instructor to complete the coursework within a period of no more than 12 months following the quarter in which the grade of Incomplete was originally given.

Academic English 20D

If you are an Academic English 20C student who needs an additional course in the Academic English 20 sequence before enrolling in Writing 39A, you may have the opportunity to enroll in Academic English 20D, a special course that gives students additional intensive language instruction tailored to their specific linguistic needs.

Comprehension Questions

1. What does it mean to hit a plateau in language development? Have you ever hit a plateau?

2. Why do some students advance quickly in learning English while others do not?

3. What types of assessments will you take in Academic English 20?

4. Guo Wei explains that when taking sit-down writing exams, it is a mistake for him to write long, sophisticated sentences with SAT words or worry about the title, conclusion, and ideas. Do you agree with Guo Wei? Why?

5. Why are timed writing exams important? What strategies can use to prepare for them?

6. What is the Academic English Diagnostic Exam? How are the results used?

7. What is a writing prompt and why is it important to learn to unpack it?

8. What is the purpose of the Progress Letter and why do you submit it at the end of the quarter?

9. What are some good ways to save your writing? What back up plan do you have in place if your computer dies in the middle of the quarter?

10. How can you track your progress and what percentage will you aim for throughout the quarter?

> " Assessment can be a powerful learning tool that helps you move forward, meet your personal learning goals and attain your objectives. The results of Academic English assessments—whether formal sit-down exams, quizzes, paper assignments, or informal feedback your instructor gives you in writing conferences—can help you discover what you need to learn or re-learn, and that is good because sometimes you'll need to slow down to address specific weaknesses so you do not fall behind later or hit a plateau in language development. "

SUPPORTING ACADEMIC HONESTY

This chapter teaches you what academic honesty* is, explains the consequences of academic dishonesty, and gives you practical tips for maintaining academic honesty.

Academic honesty is an important component of your academic experience at UCI. It will help you promote knowledge and uphold the values of the University, one of which is innovation, or the creation of original ideas.

Many people believe that borrowing others' ideas or words without crediting them is unacceptable. In the United States, for instance, intellectual property laws, including copyright* laws, protect individuals' ideas. Using someone's ideas and words without giving the original author credit is a serious violation of the law.

As a public university, abiding by the law is essential Academic honesty plays a large part in UCI's integrity. Because of this, in the first few weeks of the quarter, your Academic English 20 instructor will explain its importance and you will participate in discussions of this topic. You will learn how to summarize, paraphrase, and quote others' work. As you learn how to acknowledge their words and ideas and use the conventions for citing, your instructor will address any misunderstandings you may have. Taking positive steps to support academic honesty will help you to succeed in all your UCI courses.

This year UCI has a new academic integrity policy that goes into effect on September 1, 2016. You can find information about it from the Office of Student Conduct. See also http://www.dos.uci.edu/conduct/students/academic-integrity/index.php.

UCI takes academic honesty very seriously, and Academic English 20 instructors are required to report infractions (incidents of academic dishonesty) to Dr. Tina Matuchniak, the coordinator of academic honesty concerns, who, with the instructor, will decide if the student's academic dean should be notified, and if a letter should be placed in the student's UCI records. Offenses can result in disciplinary action (sanctions) that could include dismissal* from the university.

---

*academic honesty
(noun phrase): a code of behavior that members of an academic community follow to support such fundamental values as honesty, trust, fairness, respect, and responsibility

---

*copyright
(countable and uncountable noun): the legal right to be the only producer or seller of a book, play, film, or record for a specific amount of time. It protects written and artistic expression. Examples include: books, web sites, logos, artwork, commercials, pictorial and sculptural works, photographs, drawings, and graphic designs.

---

*dismissal
(countable and uncountable noun): being asked to leave

Academic Misconduct

According to UCI's new Academic Integrity Policy, *"Academic misconduct, in its most basic form, is gaining or attempting to gain a grade, degree, or other academic accomplishment by any means other than through your own work."* There are several forms of misconduct, including cheating, conducting acts of dishonesty, plagiarizing and collusion. Below are the descriptions of these forms, as described in information pertinent to UCI's new Academic Integrity Policy.

What Is Academic Misconduct?

Some of the common forms of academic misconduct are the following:

Cheating

- Copying from others during an exam;

- Communicating exam answers with another student during an examination;

- Offering another person's work as your own;

- Taking an examination for another student or having someone take an examination for you;

- Sharing answers from a take-home examination unless specifically authorized by the instructor:

  - If you are unsure if your instructor allows collaboration with other students, or if you are unsure about what kinds of collaboration are permitted, it is always appropriate to check with the instructor of the course;

  - Tampering with an examination after it has been corrected, then returning it for more credit;

  - Using unauthorized materials, prepared answers, written notes, or information concealed in a blue book or elsewhere during an examination;

  - Allowing others to do the research and writing of an assigned paper (including using the services of a commercial term-paper company).

Plagiarism

- Passing off as your own the ideas or words of another;

- Using a creative production without crediting the source:

  - Credit must be given for every direct quotation, for paraphrasing or summarizing a work in whole or in part, and for information which is not common knowledge.

  - Most professors at UCI use programs such as Turnitin.com to detect plagiarism. These programs are very effective and include most "paper mill" websites in their databases.

Insider Tip

Take steps to avoid participating in or being involved in academic misconduct. If your friends ask you to take exams for them, tell them, "No." Your academic future depends on your honest actions.

Collusion

- Knowingly or intentionally helping another student to perform any of the above acts of cheating or plagiarism.

Dishonest Conduct

- Stealing or attempting to steal an examination or answer key from the instructor;

- Changing or attempting to change official academic records without proper sanction;

- Submitting substantial portions of the same work for credit in more than one course without consulting all instructors involved:

- This includes reusing your own work from a previous quarter, unless the instructor has explicitly permitted you to do so;

- Forging add/drop/change cards and other enrollment documents, or altering such documents after signatures have been obtained;

- Intentionally impairing the concentration of other students and/or faculty members;

- Allowing another student to copy off your work during a test.

Source: Office of Student Conduct, http://www.dos.uci.edu/conduct/students/academic-integrity/academic-integrity-information%20for%20students.php#Defining

Insider Tip

Be aware of the consequences of being cited for participating in academic misconduct. When you are dismissed from UCI, you can no longer enroll in classes.

Engaging in Acts of Misconduct

To better understand what acts of misconduct are, let's look at what they are not. There are various ways students can be involved in acts of misconduct, even accidentally. Plagiarism is when a writer takes another writer's exact words and/or ideas and pretends they are his or her own. A writer uses them as his or her own, without giving proper credit or recognition to the original writer. Copying information from the Internet or from CliffsNotes is a type plagiarism.

Self-plagiarism is using your own writing from a previous class and handing it in again; is also considered plagiarism at UCI. That is one reason why you are required to upload your papers and other writing assignments in your Academic English 20 courses to www.turnitin.com Using turnitin.com helps you protect yourself and others in the academic community from plagiarism. The Academic English 20 instructors will explain the procedures involved in using turnitin.com and give you an enrollment password for their particular class at the turnitin.com site.

Another egregious (extremely bad and obvious) type of academic misconduct is taking friends' quizzes or tests; this type of behaviour is dishonest and wrong. Other types of academic misconduct that are also egregious and can get you into serious trouble at UCI include:

- Purchasing or "borrowing" papers, or even parts of papers
- Handing in part of a paper that you have written for a different class
- Lifting (borrowing) major parts of a paper from sources without properly citing them
- Allowing a friend to write your paper
- Allowing a peer, friend, roommate, or classmate to identify and correct your language mistakes (for example, replacing your words and sentence structures with more sophisticated ones) if you are in a language course and your instructor has told you that this practice is not acceptable
- Sharing answers to a take-home exam or quiz
- Using unauthorized materials (materials that the instructor does not allow you to use like prepared answers, written notes or information) during an exam
- Copying from others during an exam or quiz

If you have a question about UCI's Academic Integrity Policy, you may anonymously ask the Office of Student Conduct for clarification on any part of the Academic Integrity policies and procedures.

The UCI Senate Policy on Academic Honesty, Appendix VIII, explains that:

Students have responsibility for:

- Refraining from cheating and plagiarism.

- Refusing to aid or abet any form of academic dishonesty.

- Notifying professors and/or appropriate administrative officials about observed incidents of academic misconduct. The anonymity of a student reporting an incident of academic dishonesty will be protected. This means that if you report that two classmates have cheated, your identity will be protected, so your classmates will not know that you reported them.

Consequences of Academic Misconduct

In 2014-2015, a number of Academic English 20 students were dismissed (asked to leave UCI and not return) or suspended (asked to leave UCI for a short time) for using others' words as their own in their writing, for taking others' quizzes or exams, and for receiving too much help from others. Others received reprimands (official rebukes or criticism). Reports of academic misconduct remain in UCI student records for five years. Below is a short list of 2013-2014 incidents of academic misconduct, described at this website: http://honesty.uci. edu/blotter.html.

academic misconduct *(uncountable noun phrase): unacceptable or improper behavior used in an academic setting*

2013-14 Incidents of Academic Misconduct at UC Irvine

International students who are dismissed even lose their right to remain in the United States. What follows is a partial (not complete) listing of incidents of undergraduate Academic Misconduct reported to the Division of Undergraduate Education during the 2013-14 academic year.

Incident Description	Action Taken by Instructor	Action Taken by Associate Dean
Student submitted a primary source paper lacking any (reference to those whose words or ideas he or she took), thus committing (performing or being involved in) plagiarism. In a meeting with the instructor, the student also admitted to cheating on the course midterm and having another student sign in for him or her when he or she was absent from the class.	Fail Assignment	Dismissal
Student used unauthorized materials during exam.	Fail Assignment	Suspension
Student submitted the work of another student as his or her own.	Fail Course	Suspension
Student's paper was not his or her own work. At least in part, it was purchased from a vendor.	Fail Course	Suspension
Student submitted essay plagiarized from a document found online.	Fail Course	Suspension
Student had someone else use his or her ID and take an exam for them.	Fail Course and Fail Assignment	Suspension
Student submitted work from another student who had uploaded their work with answers to a website.	Other	Suspension
Student admitted to using a cell phone to look up sources during an exam, which he or she used to write half of the exam. Possible collusion (a secret agreement to do something dishonest made between two or more people), but unsubstantiated (not proved to be true).	Reprimand and Fail Assignment	Suspension
Student was found copying an essay from a student who was not supposed to be in the testing room. They sat next to each other and the student not enrolled in Academic English helped the enrolled student take his or her exam.	Reprimand, Fail Course and Fail Assignment	Suspension

"Aspire to decency. Practice civility toward one another. Admire and emulate [copy] ethical behavior wherever you find it. Apply a rigid standard of morality to your lives; and if, periodically, you fail as you surely will adjust your lives, not the standards." — Ted Koppel

What Happens if Students are Reported?

The following section is reprinted from Academic Integrity: Information for Students (http://www.dos. uci.edu/conduct/students/academic-integrity/academic-integrity-information%20for%20students.php#Defining).

For the full text of the UCI Academic Senate Procedures for Resolving Academic Integrity Policy Violations, please visit the Academic Senate website.

Students who have been reported for Academic Integrity Policy Violations are encouraged to reach out to the resources available to them:

Office of the Ombudsman: The Office of the Ombudsman acts as an independent, impartial and confidential resource. The intervention of the Ombudsman may be requested by the accused student or faculty when appropriate. The Office of the Ombudsman can assist both parties by:

- Helping the student understand his or her rights.
- Helping faculty with any questions that he or she may have relative to the student contesting the proposed sanction.
- Explaining or clarifying policy and procedures.
- Advocating for a fair process.
- For more information about the Office of the Ombudsman, please visit www.ombuds.uci.edu.

Student Academic Integrity Peer Advisors: Peer Advisors assist students in navigating the process for resolving Academic Integrity Policy Violations. They are available to provide proactive education to students who have been notified of an alleged policy violation. Peer Advisors can explain the components of the Academic Integrity process including the notification letter, the administrative meeting process, the standard of evidence used in investigations and an overview of possible sanction options. Please note that the Peer Advisor's role is to help, assist, and support the student. The role of the Peer Advisors is not to act as a spokesperson, advocate, or defense counsel for the student. To schedule a meeting with a Student Academic Integrity Peer Advisor, please e-mail scintern@uci. edu.

Procedures for Resolving Academic Integrity Policy Violations

Meeting and Decision

If you are reported for a violation of the Academic Integrity Policy, you will be asked to meet with an officer in the Office of Academic Integrity and Student Conduct to discuss the alleged violation. You do not have to attend this meeting, but if you do not, the officer will decide whether or not you have committed a violation based on the information available to them. This decision is made based on the preponderance of the evidence.

If you do attend the meeting, the officer will discuss the allegation with you and may perform additional investigation to determine what occurred. If you are found to have violated the Academic Integrity Policy, you may be assigned a sanction. Sanctions range from educational sanctions (e.g., you must attend a workshop and reflect on the experience) to dismissal from the University. For a more complete list of possible sanctions, please click here. In all cases, if you are found responsible, a record of the violation will be entered into your file with the Office of Academic Integrity and Student Conduct.

Appeal

If you are found responsible, you may appeal the decision of the Office of Academic Integrity and Student Conduct. The appeal process depends on the sanction(s) you are assigned.

For cases resulting in sanctions other than suspension or dismissal, the appeal must be based on at least one of the following grounds:

- You feel that your due process rights were violated,
- You have new evidence that would have changed the decision of the Office of Academic Integrity and Student Conduct, or
- You feel that your sanction was too harsh, given the findings of fact.

If your appeal is granted, the case will be reviewed by the Academic Integrity Review Board (AIRB). The AIRB will review all documents related to the case and come to a final determination. You cannot appeal the decision of the AIRB.

For cases resulting in a sanction of suspension or dismissal, your appeal will be heard by the Academic Integrity Review Board (AIRB). The AIRB will hold a formal hearing, in which the AIRB will review all parts of the case from the initial allegation. You will be given an opportunity to present your perspective to the AIRB. The officer from the Office of Academic Integrity and Student Conduct will also present their reasoning to the AIRB. The AIRB will make a final determination regarding the case and the proposed sanction(s). You cannot appeal the decision of the AIRB.

Possible Sanctions

The Office of Academic Integrity and Student Conduct may assign sanctions for Academic Integrity Policy Violations. Some of these sanctions are listed below:

- Educational course (e.g., requirement to attend a workshop or consultation)
- Warning
- Disciplinary probation
  - While on disciplinary probation, students may continue taking classes but may be restricted from other activities and campus privileges. Violating the terms of the probation may result in further disciplinary action, usually suspension.

- Suspension (1-3 quarters)
  - While on suspension, students may not take any classes at UCI or through UCI extension. Students will have a notation of the suspension placed on their transcript for the duration of the suspension.

- Dismissal
  - When dismissed from the University, students will receive a permanent notation of the dismissal on their transcript. Students may not participate in any campus activities after they have been dismissed.

In addition to the actions taken at the time of the incident, students who are cited for Academic Misconduct may find that:

- their admission to graduate and professional schools has been affected and they are unable to get into the graduate or professional school of their choice
- they have to return to their home countries if they are an international student

These are just a few types of academic misconduct that can get you into trouble:

Types of Academic Dishonesty	Explanation
Plagiarism	Taking words from the Internet, friends, prompts, class readings, or any other source without citing or acknowledging them
Self-Plagiarism	Taking words from your own previously submitted work
Collusion	Agreeing with others secretly to do something dishonest with others, working with someone on assignments that are to be completed alone, cheating on, or sharing information about quizzes; both the giver and the taker are at fault. Note: Any student who knowingly or intentionally helps another student in an act of academic dishonesty is guilty of collusion.
Patch Writing	Copying and rearranging materials from a variety of sources without attribution (recognizing or acknowledging that others wrote these materials and explaining where you obtained the materials)
Fraud	Falsely representing something—whether by words or conduct, by false or misleading claims, or by concealing (not revealing) what should have been disclosed; fraud is meant to deceive others. Note: Any student who does academic work for someone else or submits work completed by someone else is guilty of fraud.

Useful Words

confirm: When you confirm what you say, you are stating that you believe what you say is definitely true.

cite: When you cite words, you give the exact words of something that has been written.

commit an infraction: When you commit an infraction, you break a rule or law.

credit: When you give someone credit for their ideas and words, you are giving them credit (recognition or acknowledgement) for every direct quotation, paraphrase, or summary of a work you incorporate in your own writing, even when you rewrite their words.

pass off: When you pass off someone's writing as your own, you make people think that their writing is actually yours. This can apply to a person or a thing. Here are two examples:

- He passed himself off as a doctor. (He was not a doctor.)
- He tried to pass off his friend's writing as his own. (He tried to make others think that he wrote his own paper and that his friend did not write his paper for him.)

paraphrase: When you paraphrase, you express what someone else said or wrote in a shorter, clearer, or different way.

source: A source is a place where information or words in a new piece were originally found. Sources may include web pages as well as information in print. In Writing 39 coursework, you'll learn to create a Working Bibliography for your sources. Although your Academic English 20 instructors may not require that you identify your courses in a Work Cited page, they will expect you to identify the sources that you use in your writing, following MLA conventions.

When to Give Credit

Need to Cite	No Need to Cite
Referring to someone else's ideas, opinions, or theories, such as by paraphrasing	Using ideas that are genuinely your own
Copying exact words	Writing up your own results to a study
Reprinting or copying graphical elements such as diagrams, illustrations, maps, charts, and pictures	Including your own artwork or other original creation
Using ideas from others given in conversation, interviews, correspondence (letters or email) or heard during lectures, speeches, and from media such as television and radio	Recording anecdotes (short account or story) about people in which the people remain anonymous (unknown or unnamed)
	Using common knowledge according to accepted criteria

(adapted from Avoiding Plagiarism by Purdue University's Online Writing Lab)

Zhang Min, a former Academic English 20B student, advises,

"Ask the instructors and writing specialists at the Writing Center to give you feedbacks on "zero drafts," more earlier versions of your first draft. They gave me great suggestion. But don't just rely on them. That's no good. When you are just getting your ideas and get ready to write your first drafts, see Writing Center peer tutor or talk to a friend or a roommate about your ideas. Even if they don't know the reading materials you are going to discuss in your writing, talking to them is good idea. It can help you understand what language you'll need and the directions you'll take. All professional writer get feedback from the others. That's not cheating. But asking friends to rewrite your papers is."

> *"Regard your good name as the richest jewel you can possibly be possessed of... The way to a good reputation is to endeavor to be what you desire to appear."* —Socrates

Academic Honesty Strategies: Dos and Don'ts

Supporting academic honesty can save you time and money, lead to academic success, lower your anxiety, and most importantly even help you maintain your **integrity** (the quality of being honest and behaving in a way that is honorable). Following are some dos and don'ts to follow.

Dos

- **Do** acknowledge the sources you use in your writing.

- **Do** give yourself adequate time to complete your writing assignments.

- **Do** take advantage of campus resources that you can turn to for help if your grades are low or you feel pressured.

- **Do** remember that the anxieties or blocks you face are a normal part of the writing process.

- **Do** complete your assigned readings in English. That will help you develop the English you need to complete your writing assignments.

- **Do** take notes and annotate assigned readings in English. Pushing yourself to write in English on topics related to your writing assignments will prepare you to complete writing assignments.

- **Do** avoid classmates or others who encourage you to help them engage in academic dishonesty. If they are your friends, you will want to caution them of the consequences of academic dishonesty.

- **Do** ask your instructor for help if you are wondering whether you are engaging in (involved in) academic dishonesty.

- **Do** discuss the assigned readings with your friends and others.

- **Do** talk to your friends and others about your writing assignments and what they ask you to do.

- **Do** talk to your friends and others about your ideas pertaining to your writing assignments. This will help you clarify your ideas.

- **Do** ask those friends who have a strong command of English to help you write a list of ten to fifteen key words you might use in your writing.

- **Do** attend writing conferences with your instructor regularly.

Don'ts

- **Don't** use word for word phrases, sentences, or paragraphs of others' writing unless you quote them.

- **Don't** make slight changes in the words of others.

- **Don't** use others' thesis statements or topic sentences.

- **Don't** use a general organization plan that others have used; for instance, do not use headings or rewritten versions of others' writing. Especially avoid using the kinds of **templates** (fixed organizational plans) you may have learned previously and that agents or others may sell.

- **Don't** ask others to correct your grammar or language **errors if you are in a language course such as Academic English 20.** Do not ask others to write any part of your papers, take tests or quizzes for you, or attend class for you in any UCI course.

- **Don't** use electronic "paper mills," professional editors, or agents.

Questions & Answers

Here are some questions that past Academic English 20 writing students asked:

Q: What do **offense**, **violation** and **infraction** mean?

A: All these words refer to breaking rules or laws. A **repeated offense** means that a rule or law has been broken more than once.

Q: What does it mean if you are **dismissed** from UCI?

A: A **dismissal** is an official notice that you must permanently leave (for example, a university or a place of employment). If you are dismissed from UCI, you can no longer enroll in courses at UCI. If you are an international student with an F-1 or J-1 immigration status and you are dismissed from UCI, you are no longer able to maintain legal immigration status and you will need to transfer to another institution, change to another immigration status immediately, or leave the United States immediately.

Q: What does it mean if you are **suspended**?

A: A **suspension** is the temporary removal of a student from an academic institute for a violation of policies or rules. Suspensions are generally imposed by UCI and usually last anywhere from 1 to 3 quarters. Students on suspension are not permitted to take courses outside of UCI during this time either. This includes UCI Extension and community colleges. Any units taken during a suspension most likely will not be able to transfer back to UCI.

Q: What does it mean if you are **reprimanded**?

A: If you are **reprimanded**, you receive an official notification from an administrator that expresses disapproval of your behavior. At UCI, reprimands become a part of your official student records. You do not want to receive an official reprimand that is placed in your UCI student records, because the reprimand can negatively affect your chance of being accepted to graduate school.

Q: I've heard that I don't have to cite information that is **common knowledge.** What's that?

A: Information that does not need to be cited is that which is known by many people, is easy to learn about, and is often found in general references like dictionaries. However, even experts disagree on what constitutes **common knowledge** that does not have to be cited. When in doubt, ask your instructor.

Insider Tip

Forms are often formal contracts. Never sign contracts that you do not understand. Learning the key words in contracts will help you understand them.

The Academic Honesty, Plagiarism and Turnitin.com Form

The Academic Honesty, Plagiarism and Turnitin .com Form follows. It is critically important that you read and understand this form, as it is a contract. Your instructor will give you a copy in class and will require you to read it, sign it, and submit it. Ask questions if you do not understand any part of the form. If you would like any part of the form translated for you into a different language, please let your instructor know.

Academic Honesty, Plagiarism and Turnitin Form

Please read the following information carefully. *When you sign this form, you are confirming that you have read and understand the university's policies on academic honesty and plagiarism.*

According to the UCI Academic Senate, "Academic dishonesty is unacceptable and will not be tolerated at the University of California, Irvine." The Senate defines **academic dishonesty** as "cheating, forgery [a document copied illegally], dishonest conduct, plagiarism, and collusion in dishonest activities." **Plagiarism** is defined as intellectual theft, which means the dishonest use of the work of another person without proper citation or acknowledgment. Plagiarism in academic writing courses may take two main forms:

To steal or pass off as your own the ideas or words of another. This theft may take the form of a few words, a phrase, an extended (long) passage or an entire paper written by someone else.

To use a creative production (like an original piece of writing) without crediting the source. Sources may include web pages, as well as information in print. Credit must be given for every direct quotation, paraphrase or summary (even in your own words) of another person's work, as well as for any information that is not common knowledge.

Dishonest conduct, as defined by the academic senate, includes submitting (handing in) a paper or part of a paper a student has already received credit for in another course, even if this is the student's own work. All work given to your instructor must be original for that course. Information about UCI's policy on academic honesty and plagiarism can be viewed at http://honesty.uci.edu/students.html.

Turnitin.com: All Academic English 20 take-home writing must be uploaded to Turnitin.com. All submitted papers will be included as source documents in the Turnitin.com reference database solely for the purpose of **detecting** (discovering) plagiarism for such papers. Use of the Turnitin.com service is subject to (governed by) the Usage Policy agreement posted on the Turnitin.com site.

By signing this document, you agree that you **understand** the following forms of academic dishonesty and will **actively avoid**:

- Plagiarism (taking words from the Internet, friends, prompts, class readings or any other source without citing them or acknowledging them)

- Self-plagiarism (taking from your own previously submitted work)

- Collusion (working with someone on assignments that are to be completed alone, cheating, or sharing information about quizzes. Both the giver and the taker are at fault)

- Patch writing (copying and rearranging materials from a variety of sources without attribution)

- Fraud (doing academic work for someone or submitting work completed by someone else)

By signing this document, you agree that you understand that to protect the value of the independent work you do in this course, the work of all the students in the course may be compared for evidence of plagiarism to the work of other students, both in this course and in others, as well as other sources on the Internet and elsewhere; this involves the storage of student's work on computer systems outside of the university. Any student who withholds this permission will be assigned extra alternative work, which may include a meeting with your instructor to discuss the writing and an additional reflection paper on the process of writing this assignment. Not uploading required drafts to Turnitin.com by the assigned deadline will negatively affect your grade.

Your Name: _____

Your Signature: _____

Date: _____

A WORD OF CAUTION

It is your responsibility to ensure that the assignments you submit are free of plagiarism. This book includes instruction in the proper way to credit sources and thereby avoid plagiarism. **If you are caught plagiarizing, the plagiarized assignment will not receive credit and you may fail the course as well.**

Students' Past Attempts to Justify Participating in Academic Misconduct and Some Reasons for Their Not Working

In previous years, some students tried to get their instructors to "cut them some slack." They gave excuses for engaging in academic dishonesty. Below are their explanations and instructors' responses.

1. *I did not know what I did was wrong.* You are responsible for knowing and supporting UCI policies concerning academic honesty.

2. *My friends made me do it.* You, and you alone, are responsible for your own choices and actions. Do not let your friends coerce* you to engage in academic dishonesty.

3. *I actually wrote a perfect paper by myself outside of class; no one helped me. Even though my sit-down writing is bad, my out-of-class writing is excellent.* Your instructors agree that most students do write much better when they write outside of class. However, your instructors, more than others, know the ways you use language and rhetorical devices, your capabilities, and your **voice**. Your voice is individual and pertains to you, the writer. It's like your thumbprint. No two voices are the same and no two writers have the same voice. How you use words, how you express your attitude, and how you use your experiences and express your opinions are a part of your voice. You reveal your voice as soon as you put pen to paper in an in-class writing assignment, and it transfers to your out-of-class writing. Your voice and use of language can reliably indicate the author of papers. Be warned: the program uses automated computer services to evaluate unique writing tendencies in terms of phrasing, word choice, and other language features. What does this mean? Your instructors can often easily spot out-of-class writing that is not yours. Note too that your instructors often include writing conferences and reflection papers when they ask you to draft papers. They require you to reflect on the organization of your writing, the content of your writing, and—when appropriate—your argumentation. This helps them know your writing and enables them to recognize writing that is not yours.

4. *I was desperate. I had to cheat to get a good grade on my paper or I would not pass the course and be placed on probation.*
   Your instructors will be sorry to hear this news. They will tell you, "That's too bad. But if you were at risk of being put on probation, you should have done all you could have to support the University's academic honesty policy by getting the right kind of assistance to improve your writing."

*coerce
(verb): to use threats or orders to make someone do something he or she does not want to do. He coerced me to help him write his paper.

Paul Molinero, a former Academic English 20 student, states:

"When I was in high school, I cheated. It help me save time and get good grade without working hard. In my first quarter at UCI, I cheat just once and got caught. I feel really embarrass. All the worry made me miserable and stop me from studying for other courses. I'm lucky I was not dismiss and got to stay at UCI. My Academic English teacher was very helpful. She taught me good tips to be successful and not cheat."

Where to Go to Find More Information about UCI's Regulations Concerning Academic Misconduct

A very helpful website all students should go to is provided by the Office of Student Conduct, http://www.dos.uci.edu/conduct/students/academic-integrity/academic-integrity-information%20for%20students.php.

The information is cited directly from this website.

How to Avoid Violating the Academic Integrity Policy

Plan Your Time Appropriately

When students resort to dishonest means, it is often because they are stressed and feeling pressed for time. This is not an excuse for violating UCI's Academic Integrity Policies. Be aware of the deadlines for your assignments and exams, and set benchmarks for yourself so that you stay on top of the assignments. DO NOT PROCRASTINATE. When planning out your study time and your drafts, make sure that you also block off time for your non-academic needs. UCI's Student Wellness & Health Promotion department has excellent online resources for managing stress and maintaining balance in your life.

Use Good Study Habits

UCI's LARC office offers free 50-minute workshops on Academic Learning Skills; these workshops are useful for discovering good study habits and learning how to apply them. Using good study habits reduces your overall workload, reduces stress, and helps you to learn more effectively and efficiently.

Learn What Plagiarism Is and How to Correctly Cite

Plagiarism is one of the most common forms of academic misconduct, and it can easily be avoided. Plagiarism occurs when you submit an assignment, a part of an assignment, or a creative work as your own when it was originally created by someone else. Self-plagiarism occurs when you submit your own work for more than one class without permission from the instructors.

Please review these resources to learn how to correctly paraphrase and cite others' work in your own assignments:

- UCI Learning Module on Plagiarism
- UCI Library Introductory Guide to Citations
- Online Writing Lab (https://www.owl.english.purdue.edu/)

Reach Out for Help

Your instructor and TAs want to see you succeed in your education! If you are uncertain about the requirements for an assignment or for the course as a whole, don't be afraid to attend office hours and/or email your instructor or TAs to ask questions. Never turn to cheating as a last resort; discuss the situation with your instructors and/or TAs, and you may be able to find a solution.

Insider Tip

UCI students can take advantage of instructors' office hours as well as campus resources to improve writing and support academic honesty.

You may also find it useful to review the material on academic honesty posted on the website of the Center for Excellence in Communication and Writing: www.writingcenter.uci.edu/resources/ resources-for-students. There you will find:

- *Academic Honesty Tips:* a tip sheet on proper source citation and avoiding plagiarism, created by UCI instructors
- *Academic Honesty Learning Module:* a UCI-developed interactive multimedia learning module on academic honesty
- *Academic Honesty Learning Video:* a YouTube version of the module above

Other Campus Resources

- Center for Excellence in Communication and Writing (the Writing Center)

    – Writing Specialist Conferences

    – Peer Tutorial Sessions

- Center for Student Wellness & Health Promotion
- Counseling Center
- LARC Study Skills Workshop
- LARC Tutoring
- Videos on Academic Integrity from Simon Frasier University
- International Center
- The Academic English Resource Center

    – Grammar Workshops

    – Specialized Workshops

IUPP students can take advantage of their instructors' and IUPP academic advisors' office hours as well as the Academic English Resource Center. (See Chapter 3.)

Project Success students can also take advantage of meetings with the Project Success writing specialist or Academic English lecturer who provides them with tutorial support.

In *Knowing Language*, you will learn how to support academic honesty by crediting others' work. Practical tips for summarizing, paraphrasing, and quoting will also be described.

 "Supporting academic honesty can save you time and money, lead to academic success, lower your anxiety, and even help you maintain your integrity (the quality of being honest and behaving in a way that is honorable)."

Comprehension Questions

Academic Misconduct Scenarios

For each of these scenarios, answer the multiple-choice question and give a brief explanation of your answer.

Scenario 1: Sharon and Ming

Sharon and her friend Ming are taking Academic English 20C, but they have different instructors. One afternoon Ming asks Sharon if she has completed her first draft of paper #1, which is the same assignment for both of their classes. Sharon says that she has. Ming then asks Sharon if she can email her the draft she wrote so that she can "get some ideas" for what to write because she has not started hers. Sharon sends her the paper she wrote and Ming copies many of Sharon's words and ideas for her own paper.

1. What type of academic dishonesty has Sharon demonstrated?

    A) Plagiarism

    B) Collusion

2. Why?

Scenario 2: Min Lee

Min Lee waited to start her paper until the night before it was due. She also had math and biology homework and knew she did not have time to write her paper. She had heard about websites that sell papers and private online tutoring services that write papers for students. She decided to purchase a paper. The paper she bought was very well written and used sophisticated vocabulary. She was very careful to make sure the paper would be considered "original" by Turnitin.

1. Will Min Lee's instructor know she purchased the paper instead of writing it herself?

    A) Probably not

    B) Yes, most likely

2. Why?

Scenario 3: Mike

Mike is an Economics major in his first year at UCI. Mike is also enrolled in an Academic English 20 course, and one of the Econ essay topics is quite closely related to the topic of a paper that Mike has written for Academic English. He decides that it would spare him a great deal of work if he simply took that AE essay and added some quotes from the text assigned in his Econ course, but otherwise left the paper the same. He reasons that this is his own work, so there should be nothing wrong with submitting it in more than one course.

1. Has Mike engaged in academic dishonesty?

    A) Yes

    B) No

2. Why?

Scenario 4: Juan

Juan was patiently waiting outside of his Academic English 20C classroom with 15 other students for the instructor to arrive. The students had come to class early to prepare for a grammar quiz. As Juan studied his flashcards, he saw something that shocked him. A student named Leslie was studying an image on her iPad that looked just like the type of grammar quizzes the instructor usually gave the students. Leslie looked suspicious because she kept looking around her to make sure that the other students did not see what she was studying. Juan decided to do nothing.

1. What should Juan have done?

    A) Confronted Leslie

    B) Privately informed his instructor

    C) Continue to obviously watch Leslie so she doesn't cheat

2. Why?

Scenario 5: Louise

Louise is working hard in her Academic English course, and she has made frequent trips to the Writing Center and Peer Tutors. She just never seems to be able to come up with ideas for the assigned essay topics, which sometimes feel too abstract. As a result, she has difficulty getting started. For the final essay of the quarter, she takes the essay prompt to a writing specialist and wants to develop some ideas for the essay. The writing specialist is very encouraging and helps her brainstorm. At one point, the writing specialist makes a suggestion that Louise ought to think about the topic using a particular metaphor. Louise decides that this metaphor fits perfectly and decides to use it in the introduction paragraph of her paper.

1. Is borrowing a particular metaphor an act of plagiarism?

    A) Yes

    B) No

2. Why?

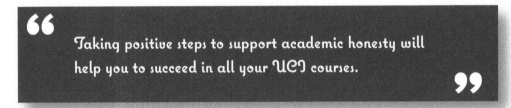

> *Taking positive steps to support academic honesty will help you to succeed in all your UCI courses.*

CHAPTER FIVE

MANAGING YOUR TIME AT UCI

Percival V. Guevarra

When students get to UCI, they often soon discover that they need to improve their time management skills. No longer are high school teachers and others helping them schedule their time. Many find that at UCI they are not in classes and structured extracurricular activities all day long as they were in high school. At UCI, they have the freedom to spend much of their time as they like.

This chapter teaches you the importance of managing your time wisely and explains possible challenges to time management. It also describes activities that will help you prioritize your tasks in order to maximize your personal efficiency at UCI.

Time Management

Time management refers to a range of skills, tools, and techniques that people use to accomplish specific tasks, projects, or goals. To help you understand the importance of effective time management, consider the following scenario.

Imagine it is dinnertime and you are with a group of friends. You all decide to find a good restaurant. When you enter the restaurant and tell the host that you would like a table, the host asks how many people are in your group. However, you realize that you are missing one friend because the person is late. The host says you must wait until everyone is present, even though the restaurant will close in one hour.

Luckily, your friend arrives 30 minutes before the restaurant closes and you are able to get a table. Everyone except your friend quickly decides what to order, but your late friend cannot stop looking at his phone. Unfortunately, time passes and the waiter tells you that the restaurant is closing, and he cannot take your order. Everyone leaves the restaurant and decides to go home. Later, you decide not to invite your friend to spend time with you anymore.

Time management is important for you and the people around you. Managing your time helps you stay productive and accomplish what you want to do. The way you manage your time also tells others what kind of person you are and whether they can trust you. When you do not manage your own time effectively, it can negatively impact those around you and undermine their ability to obtain their own objectives. And, as seen above, it can result in people becoming upset or unhappy with you. These reasons make time management very important for succeeding in both college and in life. This chapter will provide strategies and activities for managing time effectively. To make best use of these activities, try them early and in the order they are presented.

Procrastination

Everyone procrastinates. That is, they put off or delay something that must be done. This might be because they are too busy, feel unmotivated or unprepared, or believe they receive the best results when waiting until the last minute. Regardless, procrastination has consequences. However, there are a myriad* of ways to combat this common bad habit:

*myriad
(adjective): an indefinitely large number

*accountable
(adjective): responsible

- Split your task into smaller, more achievable tasks.

- Form study groups, or ask others to help you stay accountable*.

- Give yourself reasonable amounts of time to work, and remember to take breaks.

- Work in productive environments that are away from distractions.

Finding Your Starting Point

The first step in making progress in achieving an objective is to understand its importance to you, where you are at the beginning of the task, and where you want to be at the end of the task. This is your starting point. Consider the objective of studying for a test. If you need to review test material, you will want to consider how important studying for the test is to you, which material you have you already mastered, and which material you will need to master to do well on the test. Consider the objective of increasing the time you spend studying in general. As a starting point, you will want to examine how much time you currently spend studying.

The "wheel of life" activity (Figure 5.1) will give you a broader perspective of your starting point for increasing the time you spend studying. This activity helps you to determine how satisfying it is to participate in a variety of activities and helps you begin to prioritize the amount of time you spend studying and engaging in other tasks. When you prioritize, you put tasks, objectives, etc. into their order of importance, so that you can deal with the most important first. Each section of the wheel represents a different category, and coloring a section represents satisfaction in that category.

"The bad news is time flies. The good news is you're the pilot."

– Michael Altshuler

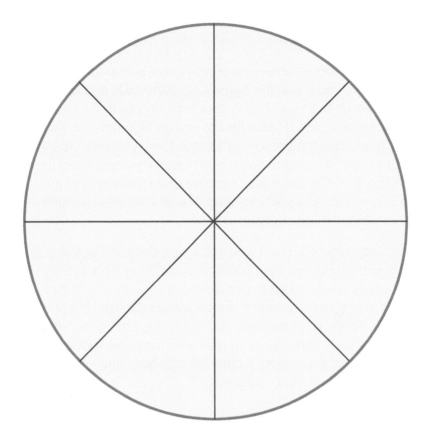

Figure 5.1 The Wheel of Life

- Homework
- Studying
- Clubs
- Family
- Fun/Recreation

- Social Life/Relationships
- Work
- Money
- Class 1, 2, 3, etc.
- Health/Rest

Directions for Using the Wheel Life

To help you get started on the task of better using your time, try using the Wheel of Life. Label the sections of the wheel with different categories and color them in based on your satisfaction. If you are completely satisfied, color the entire section. If you are half satisfied, color half of the section. For example, you could color an entire section labeled "engineering class," but only half of a section labeled "English class." This means that you are less satisfied with English class and may want to spend more time making progress in English than in engineering. Try making your own wheel of life by labeling and coloring the sections. Below the wheel are some sample categories for sections that you might consider.

When labeling the sections, you will want to consider the following questions:

- What contributes to your overall satisfaction?

- What takes away from your overall satisfaction?

- What is the ideal balance?

- What do you want to change?

Prioritizing

After getting an idea of where you are and where you want to be, an important next step is to prioritize how important each item is. You will need to consider the importance of the task to you immediately and in the long term. For example, you may be less satisfied about your progress in Calculus than in Engineering, but if you have a midterm in your Engineering class tomorrow, it might be more important for you to prioritize studying for the engineering class than the calculus class at this moment.

Table 5.1 contains a prioritization chart to help you prioritize your tasks at UCI this week. List the tasks you have, and then circle the importance of the task to help you prioritize which task to work on first. To make this prioritizing activity more effective, try splitting up large tasks into small ones. For example, a research paper can be split into researching, planning, and drafting. It may also be helpful to consider due dates, difficulty of the task, and the length of time needed to complete the task.

Table 5.1: Priority Chart

Importance	Task	✔ (Complete)
___ High ___ Medium ___ Low		
___ High ___ Medium ___ Low		
___ High ___ Medium ___ Low		
___ High ___ Medium ___ Low		
___ High ___ Medium ___ Low		

Setting Goals

Many UCI students are familiar with making to-do lists, in which they list all the tasks they need to accomplish by a specific deadline. By now, you are familiar with being able to prioritize those lists. However, a number of students stop there and procrastinate. This is in part because of what they list—broad goals or goals that cannot be clearly defined. For example, they might list the goal of "doing homework." "Doing homework" may refer to homework for several classes, several assignments, or even several types of activities. When students decide to spend time "doing homework," they may not know how much time to give to the task. They may spend two hours doing homework, become overwhelmed by the actual amount of work involved, lose motivation, and then decide to procrastinate.

Being able to set goals effectively is a skill. When people are able to do this, they increase their confidence and chances of success, which ultimately improves time management overall. One strategy for this is known as developing **SMART goals.** SMART is an acronym that stands for different criteria.

SMART

Specific—When and where will it happen, and who will be involved?

Measurable—How will I track my progress?

Action-oriented—What will happen?

Realistic—Based on the time this will take and the time I have, is this a realistic goal?

Time-sensitive—What is my deadline?

Table 5.2 is an example of the general goal of "studying" revised as a SMART goal. Students can use the chart below to write their own goals, filling in the additional rows in the chart.

Table 5.2: SMART Chart

Goal	Specific	Measurable	Action-Oriented	Realistic	Time-sensitive	Confidence level & ways to increase confidence
Study	Study for Biology class at the library	Study for Biology class at the library for 4 hours	Review Biology notes & read textbook at the library for 4 hours	Review Bio notes for 1 hour, read textbook for 1 hour at the library	Review Bio notes 1 hour before dinner, read textbook 1 hour after dinner at the library by Thursday	*90% confident* -prepare notes in advance -study w/ a partner -avoid social media

Insider Tip

Make Time for Yourself!

• Exercise, socialize, and get your sleep.

• Reward yourself for your efforts. Diligent studying for four hours followed by a half-hour phone call to your best friend is more productive than four or five hours of studying interrupted by brief text messages

• Study with a group or meet a friend to study.

• Treat yourself to breakfast before a study session.

Planning Your Time

Even SMART goals can fail if students do not think about the amount of time they will need to accomplish goals and schedule time to complete them. Consider, for instance, those students who plan to do all their homework on Sunday and spend Saturday with friends. This is not a good idea, since students cannot stay productive for eight hours consecutively (in a row) without breaks, even with a SMART goal. Planning when you will work and for how long is just as important and making a SMART goal. Planning your schedule in reverse can be particularly useful.

To plan a schedule in reverse, begin with a blank weekly schedule. Start by filling in the time slots that you know are unavailable. This may be because you are attending class or involved in specific UCI activities. These unavailable times are usually predictable because they are part of a routine that you do not have much control over, since classes and activities are scheduled by other people, not you. After filling in the busy time slots, fill in the time slots for activities that are flexible. These are activities that happen every day, and you are in control of when they happen. They can include eating, getting ready in the morning for class, sleeping, going to the gym or working out, and possibly commuting. The final step for planning in reverse is to look at the blank spaces in your schedule, and evaluate the best times for your activity. By planning a schedule in this way, you can improve both productivity and time management (Table 5.3).

Weekly Agenda (Table 5.3)

	Sunday	Monday	Tuesday	Wednesday	Thursday	Friday	Saturday
8am							
9am							
10am							
11am							
12pm							
1pm							
2pm							
3pm							
4pm							
5pm							
6pm							
7pm							
8pm							
9pm							
10pm							
11pm							

Directions for Using a Weekly Agenda

1. Fill in slots with unavailable times, such as class.

2. Fill in slots with flexible times, such as eating and sleeping.

3. Use the remaining slots to fill in the times that you plan to make progress towards your goal.

Yeng Li, a former Aademic English 20C student, offers this advice:

"Write everything down. Don't just think you'll remember due dates. Carry around and use a quarter planner to indicate when your assignments are due, exams are given, writing conferences are given and events are held. Copy important deadlines (tests, papers due) into your planner from your syllabi. Even write down deadlines of all drafts of papers, for instance, zero draft, 1st draft, 2nd draft, final draft."

Bowen Qi, a former Academic English 20B student, remarks:

"Don't waste time between classes and meetings. You can use small bits of time to your advantage. With just a little time, you can review, edit, and revise your notes from a recent lecture. With ten minutes, you can even revise one of the paragraphs of a paper or answer some math problems."

Managing Distractions

Distractions, which cause you not to pay attention to something, constitute a major hindrance to time-management. These can vary from person to person. Some students are distracted by the noise in a lively café and prefer to work in a quiet library, while others may find a library's silence distracting. Some students prefer to work on a laptop, while others find that they spend more time checking e-mail and reading social media when working on a laptop. Some students prefer to work at night when everyone else is asleep, while others cannot focus beyond a certain hour. Whether the distraction is something external or internal, it is important to know what distracts you specifically.

Insider Tip

Consider your energy levels and productivity when scheduling the times you want to make progress on achieving your goal.

Consider the need to take breaks. You may want to schedule breaks every two hours.

External Distractions

External distractions may come from objects, people, or your environment. Specifically, these might include:

- Smart phones, computers, or the internet in general

- Roommates or friends

- Noise, or lack thereof, in your environment

- Internal distractions may come from your emotions, motivation, or energy levels. For example:
  - Excitement from an upcoming event or depression from a recent event
  - Not wanting to do the activity or thinking it is stupid
  - Fatigue early in the morning or at the end of the day

Tips for Managing Distractions

- Work in an environment that is productive for you.
- Schedule work at a time that is productive for you.
- Seek assistance from others to keep you on task and away from distraction.
- Limit the objects to the necessities. Do you need the internet? Do you need your phone?
- Take breaks at regular intervals* and celebrate successes.

*interval
(countable noun): a period of time between things

Taking breaks is especially important, even if it feels like "wasted" time. Taking breaks helps manage distractions and avoid fatigue. When students take breaks at regular intervals, they can stay focused on small parts of a task and the tasks that need to be done and the tasks that can wait. By setting aside what can wait, students are less prone* to distraction, thus maximizing productivity. One well-known strategy for setting a schedule with breaks is the Pomodoro technique.

*prone
(adjective): having a tendency to do something

The Pomodoro Technique

The Pomodoro technique involves repeating the following steps:

1. Decide on a task that you want to accomplish.

2. Set a timer for 25 minutes.

3. Work on the task for 25 minutes.
   - If you start getting off-task, write a short note about the distraction on a separate paper, and then keep working on your task.

4. After 25 minutes of work, take a 3-5 minute break.

5. Do steps 2-4 three more times.

6. After four intervals, take a longer 15-30 minute break.

The goal of the Pomodoro technique is to create a habit of focusing on a task for 25 minutes, while minimizing distractions and staying productive. It can be applied to doing homework, studying for tests, or writing an essay.

Insider Tip

Plan Your Study Space

Study in a place where you are free from distractions. For example, if you are distracted at the library, try studying at home or in a coffee shop.

Jia Wong, a former Academic English student, offers this advice:

"Learn to make tough decisions and stick by them. When I had a difficult paper to write, I canceled meetings with friends and postponed long conversations home. I concentrated on writing my paper instead. I postponed coffee dates and made lots of sacrifices. At the end of the quarter, I had a high grade point average. My sacrifices had paid off."

Similar to learning a language, managing time requires practice. Try the strategies you have never used and continue to use the strategies that work well for you. Some of these strategies may involve working with others in order to stay on task and be accountable. If a strategy is not working for you, even though it works for others, try to approach the task in a different way. The more aware you are of your starting point—where you are at the beginning of the task, your goal, and the obstacles in between—the easier time management will be.

Comprehension Questions

1. What are the advantages of effective time management and how can effective time management give you control over your life, reduce your stress, and help you accomplish specific objectives?

2. Time management refers to a range of skills, tools, and techniques that people use to accomplish specific tasks, projects, or goals. Which skills, tools and techniques have you found most effective in managing your time at UCI?

3. Do you believe that being busy can actually help you manage your time more effectively? Why? Does it help you stay more organized or keep your priorities in order?

4. What can you do to avoid staying up at night?

5. What challenges can prevent you from working on tasks of the highest priority first?

6. Which studying tasks take you the greatest amount of time? Should they? How can you do these tasks more efficiently?

7. How do you deal with interruptions when trying to complete your homework assignments?

8. Is it a good idea to get unpleasant chores completed as soon as possible? Why?

9. How can you make your study area a pleasant place to work? Can you find what you need without wasting time?

10. How can you prevent classmates or friends from wasting your time?

"Time is the most valuable coin in your life. You and you alone will determine how that coin will be spent. Be careful that you do not let other people spend it for you."

— Carl Sandburg

CHAPTER SIX

USING CAMPUS RESOURCES

UCI offers a wealth of resources to help make your time rewarding and enjoyable. Throughout your time at UCI, you'll have multiple opportunities to take advantage of them. As you become familiar with UCI, you'll want to take every opportunity to make new friends, obtain new experiences, and grow as an individual. Many of the resources the campus provides will help you learn English and develop your ability to write. Others help you achieve academic excellence and adapt to campus life. The following list includes important campus resources and offices.

The Academic English Program and Class Resources

Your Instructor

One of your best resources is your Academic English 20 instructor. Your instructor keeps regular office hours each week set aside for drop-in visits. Appointments can also be made with your instructor to meet at a different time. Your instructor's office hours can be found on the class syllabus. Academic English instructors do *not* have office phones, so if you need to reach your instructors, you can contact them via email as listed on the course syllabus. You can find instructors' and classmates' emails by using UCI's campus directory, which can be found at the top of UCI's home page at http://www.uci.edu/.

Insider Tip

For a productive drop-in session with your instructor, always come prepared. Bring something you have written or your assignment and questions you want to ask and topics you want to cover.

Academic English Program Office
http://www.humanities.uci.edu/esl

You may need to visit the Academic English Program Office if you have an enrollment issue and want to speak to the Office Manager in person or need to speak to the Director of the Program. The Program Office is located in Humanities Instructional Building 335.

Writing Resources

Center for Excellence in Writing and Communication
193 Ayala Science Library
(949) 824-8949
http://www.writingcenter.uci.edu

The UCI Center for Excellence in Writing and Communication (Writing Center) is an instructional service that promotes effective writing and communication as lifelong skills. Its focus is on the writer and the writing process. During your consultation, expect to be actively engaged in long-term writing improvement, including learning strategies for identifying errors and revising. The Writing Center is not an editing service. Students cannot drop papers off for "fixing."

The Writing Center's services include:

Appointments

Students can set up an appointment with an experienced writing specialist if they want to get in-depth feedback for any kind of writing they are working on, or if they just want to brainstorm. This is best done well in advance of deadlines.

Tips for Appointments:

- Appointment slots are only available up to 2 weeks in advance and fill up fast. Check back regularly for new availability.

- Make your appointment far enough in advance of a due date to allow enough time for revision.

- Complete the intake form before your appointment to make more efficient use of the time.

- Bring questions. You will learn more effectively if you are actively engaged in revision.

Online Consultations

Online consultations are available for students who may be unable to come to campus for an appointment or who simply prefer electronic correspondence over in-person assistance. When submitting a draft for an online consultation, students must e-mail a prompt and no more than two specific things they would like feedback on. Response time will depend on the volume of submissions during the quarter.

Peer Tutoring

Students can drop-in at one of four locations (Langson Library, Science Library, Mesa Court, Middle Earth) to see a peer tutor on a first-come, first-served basis. Peer tutors have undergone a training course and meet weekly with a professional coordinator. No advance appointment with a peer tutor is necessary. However, it is best to come early to avoid long wait times. For peer tutor hours and locations during the quarter, visit http://www.writingcenter.uci.edu/peer-tutors.

Services

The International Center

G302 Student Center
(949) 824-7249, Fax: (949) 824-3090
http://www.ic.uci.edu

The International Center supports UCI's international population through a variety of programs designed to enhance both academic and personal experiences in the U.S. The International Center offers credit-courses, workshops, advising, immigration services, social events, and travel and employment opportunities.

COURSES

International Students Transition to Educational and Personal Success (I-STEPS) Course

I-STEPS is a 1.3 unit, 10-week course created especially for new, first-year, international students that meets once a week for one hour and provides them with the following opportunities:

- Learn about American culture in a comfortable environment
- Gain guidance on how to succeed academically and socially at UCI
- Build a network of friends, staff, and faculty at UCI
- Explore on-campus resources and services

The English Conversation Program

The English Conversation Program is a 1.3 unit course that builds English skills by fostering personal interaction between UCI students of all cultures in a fun, friendly, and casual environment. English facilitators assist international students with improving their English conversation skills through one-on-one partner and group activities and interesting discussions. The program provides an opportunity for both international students and English facilitators to:

- Develop cultural insights
- Build relationships
- Recognize the value of our diverse campus community

WORKSHOPS

Career Development Workshop Series

Career Development workshops provide international students with information on how to obtain on- and off-campus jobs and internships in addition to teaching students how to search for jobs, information on employment and work visas, and American workplace etiquette. Previous workshops have included Interview Techniques, Professional Networking, and Writing Professional Emails.

The English Development Workshops

The English Development Workshops can enhance your speaking and academic writing in English. Sessions are hosted by representatives from the Program in Academic English and the Writing Center. Previous topics have included idioms, body language, creative writing, and presentation skills. Your instructors will contact you about these workshops.

PROGRAMS & ACTIVITIES

Bye-Bye Culture Shock

Bye-Bye Culture Shock is a drop-in discussion group that eases the transition process for international students. This group provides a safe and private space to share experiences and get support on a variety of topics, such as cultural adjustment, confidence, identity, past experiences, and future goals.

Across the Bridge: Diversity Dialogue

An excellent way to develop new friends while practicing English and exploring your ideas is to participate in Across the Bridge conversations. International and domestic students engage in open conversations about diversity in America, as well as discuss personal identities that include cultural backgrounds and experiences. The conversations are co-hosted by the Cross-Cultural Center and the Study Abroad Center. Previous topics have included Festivals and Celebrations, Exploring Gender Roles, and Education Around the World.

Life in the United States Series

These workshops address a variety of topics that help international students learn about American culture. Topics in the past have included "How to Make an American Friend," "Dating and Relationships," "Finding Housing in Irvine," and "American Pop Culture."

Helping Hands Program

The Helping Hands Program provides students with the opportunity to give back to the community through service projects. Domestic and international students volunteer to work together at various sites in the community. They participate in such activities as beach clean-ups, food drives, and home visitations to the elderly.

Explore Southern California Trips

What better way to learn about American culture than to visit interesting places in Southern California? The International Center hosts various trips throughout the year to local points of interest around Southern California. Trips in the past have included the Getty Museum, the Griffith Observatory, Santa Monica Beach, and Little Saigon.

International Coffee Hour

The International Coffee Hour is an opportunity for international and domestic students to socialize in a comfortable environment about any topic. Refreshments are provided.

For dates and times for these and even more programs, visit www.ic.uci.edu.

RESOURCES

Jack Langson Library (Adjacent to Aldrich Hall)
P.O. Box 19557, Irvine, CA 92623-9557
(949) 824-6836
http://www.lib.uci.edu

The Jack Langson Library supports the arts, humanities, social science, education, and business and management.

The Reference and Government Information Desk on the first floor provides reference assistance and information on a variety of topics to campus and community users. You will find a series of reference guides in paper and electronic format to help you research both general and specialized topics.

Ayala Science Library

(Across from Steinhaus Hall)
P.O. Box 19557, Irvine, CA 92623-9557
(949) 824-6836
http://www.lib.uci.edu

The Science Library houses the science, medicine, and technology collections including material in the fields of astronomy, biology, chemistry, computer science, earth systems science, engineering, mathematics, medicine, and physics. The Science Library provides more than 2,000 individual study spaces, faculty and graduate reading rooms, more than 50 group study rooms, and an extended-hours study center. In the Reference Room on the second floor, expert staff is available for research assistance and consultation, and computer workstations provide access to a vast array of electronic journals, research databases, and other Internet resources.

Academic Testing Center

3040 Anteater Instructional Research Building
(949) 824-6207
http://www.testingcenter.uci.edu

UCI's Academic Testing Center administers placement tests to new and continuing students. It also administers other language tests for exemptions from general education categories VI and VIII. For more information on placement testing and summer testing dates, visit the Academic Testing Center website or call the Center's office.

Freshman Seminar Program

611C Aldrich Hall
(949) 824-1955
http://www.freshmanseminar.uci.edu

Small seminars are offered to new freshmen students to introduce them to the academic culture of UC Irvine. In these seminars, students learn about topics of current interest in sections of up to 15 students. Freshman Seminars (University Studies 3 classes) are offered all three quarters, with priority given to new students who can enroll in a maximum of three sections during their time at UCI.

International Peer Group

674 Aldrich Hall
(949) 824-6776
http://www.isep.due.uci.edu

The International Peer Group's (IPG) mission is to assist UCI's international freshmen in making a smooth transition into university life. IPG provides both academic and social support in order to engage international students in UCI's vibrant campus life and help them create solid relationships in their new environment. In addition to individual mentoring, IPG offers small group meetings and larger group events during Welcome Week and throughout the year. Students with questions or who do not yet have a mentor should contact the office.

Learning and Academic Resource Center

284 Rowland Hall
(949) 824-6451
http://www.larc.uci.edu, larc@uci.edu

The Learning and Academic Resource Center (LARC) provides academic support programs for undergraduate students. These include course-specific tutorials, as well as Academic Learning Skills workshops on specific study skills (e.g., time management, academic reading, and preparation for exams). Tutorials involve informal review sessions in which 12-15 students enrolled in the same lecture compare notes, discuss readings, develop organizational tools, and predict test items in two, 50-minute LARC Sessions per week. For more information about the tutorials, visit LARC's website.

Peer Academic Advising Program

256 Aldrich Hall
(949) 824-2367
http://www.due.uci.edu/paap/

The Peer Academic Advising Program provides academic counseling based not only on academic, but also personal experiences of UCI students. Peer academic advisors (PAAs) are juniors and seniors who manage issues related to academic counseling and have a wide knowledge of campus resources available to students, such as the Career Center, Office of Disability Services, Financial Aid, Housing, and the Learning and the Academic Resource Center (LARC). They have regular office hours in their respective academic units. They assist students in selecting courses to best fit their college and career paths, planning quarterly programs of study, learning about the various majors and minors, obtaining information about UCI's resources and opportunities, and adjusting to life as UCI undergraduates.

OPPORTUNITIES

Study Abroad Center

1100 Student Services II
(949) 824-6343
http://www.studyabroad.uci.edu, studyabroad@uci.edu

The Study Abroad Center is a comprehensive resource and counseling center that helps students take advantage of the many worldwide opportunities that exist for study, work, internship, volunteering, research, and non-credentialed teaching that relates to their degree programs at UCI.

Students are advised to plan early in their academic career in order to best match studying abroad with their major to graduate on time. Programs are available for students in every major. Participation in study abroad satisfies category VIII, international/global issues, of the UCI general education requirement. Students are encouraged to study abroad as a sophomore or junior, allowing the opportunity to incorporate their international learning into their final year at UCI.

Undergraduate Research Opportunities Program
2300 Student Services II
(949) 824-4189
http://www.urop.uci.edu, urop@uci.edu

The Undergraduate Research Opportunities Program (UROP) encourages and facilitates research and creative activities by undergraduates. UROP offers assistance to students and faculty through all phases of the research activity: proposal writing, developing research plans, resource support,

conducting the research and analyzing data, and presenting results of the research at the annual spring UCI Undergraduate Research Symposium. Calls for proposals are issued in the fall and spring quarters. Projects supported by UROP may be done at any time during the academic year and/ or summer. In addition, all students participating in faculty-guided research activities are welcome to submit their research papers for faculty review and possible publication in the annual *UCI Undergraduate Research Journal*.

UROP also sponsors the following programs:
- Biophotonic Summer Undergraduate Research Program (B-SURP)
- Edwards Life Sciences Summer Undergraduate Research Program (E-SURP)
- Integrated Micro/Nano Summer Undergraduate Research Experience (IM-SURE)
- Inter-Disciplinary Summer Undergraduate Research Experience (ID-SURE)
- Multidisciplinary Design Program (MDP)
- Summer Undergraduate Research Fellowship in Information Technology (SURF-IT)
- Summer Undergraduate Research Program (SURP)

Complete information on current UROP programs can be found on the UROP website. For additional questions, contact UROP in person, telephone or by e-mail.

Wang Xiuying, a former Academic English 20B student, states,

"UROP enabled me to do research as an undergraduate. I even got to present this research at a symposium. I had lots of one-on-one contact with my professor."

Li Na, a former Academic English 20A student, advises,

"Every time I got confused about whether I was meeting my degree requirements or needed help with my course schedule, I went to my academic counselor. I prepared by bringing questions. My counselor was great and even helped me figure out how many units to take."

Academic Advising Offices

You should see an academic counselor when you have a question about your academic goals and choices at UCI. There may be times when you are feeling confused or overwhelmed or generally unclear about what you are supposed to be doing. Counselors can assist you in selecting courses to meet your career goals, in learning about various majors and minors, in goal setting and exploration, in making sure you are on track to graduate, in developing strategies to improve your academic performance, in getting questions answered about policies and procedures, and in obtaining referrals and advice about campus resources. Here at UCI, our majors are housed in academic schools. Below is a list of Academic Advising Offices. From the websites, you can find staff names and email addresses.

School	Telephone	Web Site
Claire Trevor School of the Arts	949-824-6646	http://www.arts.uci.edu
Francisco J. Ayala School of Biological Sciences	949-824-5318	http://www bio.uci.edu
The Paul Merage School of Business	949-824-1609	http://www merage.uci.edu
Campuswide Honors Program (CHP)	949-824-5461	http://www.honors.uci.edu
School of Education	949-824-5118	http://www education.uci.edu
The Henry Samueli School of Engineering	949-824-4334	http://www.engineering.uci.edu
School of Humanities	949-824-5132	http://www.humanities.uci.edu/SOH
Donald Bren School of Information and Computer Science	949-824-5156	http://www.ics.uci.edu
Program in Nursing Science	949-824-1514	http://www.nursing.uci.edu
Department of Pharmaceutical Sciences	949-824-1991	http://www.pharmsci.uci.edu
School of Physical Sciences	949-824-6507	http://www.ps.uci.edu
Programs in Public Health	949-824-2358	http://www.publichealth.uci.edu
School of Social Ecology	949-824-6861	http://www.socialecology.uci.edu
School of Social Sciences	949-824-6803	http://www.socsci.uci.edu
Division of Undergraduate Education (Undecided/Undeclared)	949-824-6987	http://www.uu.uci.edu

Wang Xiuying, a former Academic English 20C student, explains:

"If it had not been for my academic counselor, I would never be able to graduate on time with my classmates."

Undecided/Undeclared Advising Program

256 Aldrich Hall, (949) 824-6987
http://www.due.uci.edu/uu

Students who enter the University as freshmen or sophomores may be uncertain about which major they should choose and may not feel ready to declare their major or even to identify their interests with a particular school. Such students participate in the Undecided/Undeclared Advising Program, which is administered by the Division of Undergraduate Education. The goal of the Undecided/Undeclared Advising Program is to help students make the best informed and most rational choice of a major that is possible. All students at UCI are required to choose their major by the time they reach junior status.

Housing and Transportation

Housing Office and Housing Administration

Housing Administrative Services: G458 Student Center
(949) 824-6811
http://www.housing.edu/och

At UCI, there are two housing office locations to assist students with their housing needs.

The office in room G465 of the Student Center provides students with information about on- and off- campus housing options at UCI. In order to aid students in finding housing off-campus, computerized listings of apartments and houses for rent, rooms for rent in private homes, roommates wanted, and roommates available are maintained by the office. Additionally, the housing staff conducts any outreach progress to prospective students, such as tours of our on-campus residence halls and the Stay Over Program.

Housing Administrative Services serves many administrative functions in addition to providing general housing information. Students submit on-campus housing applications and contracts to this office, as well as make housing rent payments to the housing cashier.

On-Campus Housing

UCI offers housing options for all new students. There is an online application process and you must meet deadlines. The Student Housing website has detailed information about what to do and when to apply for housing on campus. See **www.housing.uci.edu**

Off-Campus Housing

If you decide to live off campus, the Student Housing Office can assist you.

Transportation

Without a doubt, travel is one of the greatest ways to explore Orange County and see the United States. While at UCI, you'll find the following resources helpful:

The Anteater Express

The Anteater Express provides transportation services from UCI to nearby locations.

515 Bison Modular, Irvine, CA 92697, (949) 824-5547
http://www.shuttle.uci.edu/

Find additional UC Irvine transportation resources at www.paring.uci.edu/AT.

The Orange County Transportation Authority

Visit http://www.octa.net/Index.aspx, an online resource with up-to-date transportation information. The Plan My Bus or Rail Trip link makes your planning easy.

UCI Affiliate Discount for Prime Time Airport Shuttle

How does it work? UCI has negotiated a discount with Prime Time Shuttle for transportation **to and from UCI campus.** If you would like to be picked up/dropped off somewhere other than on the UCI campus, please contact Prime Time Shuttle via the "Comments" section to check if there are additional fees.

- Rates:
  To/From John Wayne Airport: $9 one-way
  To/From Los Angeles International: $20 one-way

*When companies negotiate these deeply discounted rates, they usually take it out of the driver's cut, so *please tip generously!*

- Book Your Ride
  Visit Prime Time Shuttle's UCI Affiliate Discount Page.|Select UCI under "School" as your pick-up or drop-off location.
  Enter your address into the "comments" section on the reservation page.

Safety

Safety Escorts
http://www.police.uci.edu/services/safety-escorts/index.html/
(949) 824-SAFE (7233)

The Police Department offers a FREE Safety Escort Service. By calling, you can arrange to have a trained escort meet you at your location and accompany you to your destination. Safety Escorts are available 24 hours a day to all campus locations as well as several location off campus. You may also pre-arrange an escort.

Driving in the United States

If you plan to drive in California, you must obtain a California Driver License from the Department of Motor Vehicles (DMV). International students must complete iNavigate UCI (International Center Ceck-In process) before applying. They will need to present their passport, I-20, DS-2019 visa document, and I-94 document. They will be required to take a driving and written test. They should schedule an appointment in advance by visiting http://www.dmv.gov

Insider Tip

Review the Driver License Handbook (available in various languages) www.dmv.ca.gov/pubs/pubs.htm.

Department of Motor Vehicles near UC Irvine

Costa Mesa
650 W. 19th Street

Costa Mesa, CA 92627

Santa Ana
1330 East First Street

Santa Ana, CA 92701

Laguna Hills
23535 Moulton Pkwy.

Laguna Hills, CA 92653

Student Life and Well-Being

Career Center
100 Student Services I
(949) 824-6881, Fax: (949) 824-2294
http://www.campusrec.uci.edu

Do you know what you want to be? Or maybe you haven't even decided upon a major? Working with a career counselor can help you. Do you know you would have to pay several hundred dollars to a counselor in private industry for the same services provided to you by the Career Center? Take advantage of their professional services today. Make an individual appointment in the Career Center or sign up for a workshop online. Don't leave your future to chance.

Campus Recreation
680 California Avenue
(949) 824-5346
http://www.campusrec.uci.edu

The Anteater Recreation Center (ARC) has facilities such as basketball courts, racquetball courts, a swimming pool, rock climbing wall, and many more.

Associated Students of the University of California, Irvine (ASUCI)
G244 Student Center
(949) 824-5547, Fax: (949) 824-2010
http://www.asuci.uci.edu

The Associated Students of the University of California, Irvine provide a forum for expression of student views and interests, encourage and maintain the freedom to pursue knowledge, encourage student academic rights and responsibilities, represent and articulate student rights to a voice in campus governance and foster recognition of the rights of students in this university community.

Bookstore: The Hill
210-B Student Center
(949) 824-4455, Fax: (949) 824-8545
http://www.thehill.uci.edu

Conveniently located in the Student Center, the Hill is UCI's not-for-profit bookstore. The store is students' one-stop shop for course materials, general books, UCI apparel, gifts, school supplies, and more.

Student Life and Leadership and Dean of Students
UCI Dean of Students, G308 Student Center
(949) 824-5181, Fax: (949) 824-3412
http://www.dos.uci.edu

The mission of the Office of the Dean of Students is to provide services, programs, and facilities that enhance the quality of education by extending the learning environment beyond the classroom and into the co-curricular lives of UCI students. The Office of the Dean of Students promotes student participation in campus life and advocates for needs that are valued by students and validated by campus objectives.

Cross-Cultural Center
103 Gateway, Cross-Cultural Center
(949) 824-7215, Fax: (949) 824-3056
http://www.ccc.uci.edu

The Cross-Cultural Center is dedicated to supporting the diversity of UCI's students, staff, and faculty. Their mission is to provide a network of support services which support the personal, social, cultural, and academic well-being of UCI's ethnic and culturally diverse students and to promote the education and celebration of a multi-ethnic, multicultural campus community.

Student Health Center
501 Student Health, Irvine, CA 92697-5200
(949) 824-5301
http://www.shs.uci.edu

The UCI Student Health Center provides:
- Comprehensive primary care for health and wellness with an emphasis on personal sensitivity and attention to individual patient needs
- Convenient consultation and treatment in selected health specialties
- First aid and urgent care for the entire campus community and treatment for work related injuries to faculty, administration, staff and campus visitors
- Medical surveillance and recommendations for the campus on a range of health promotion and disease prevention initiatives
- Crisis consultation and outreach services to the campus community

The Student Health Center is open 8:00am-5:00pm, Monday-Friday. Regular services provided at Student Health include: primary care and specialty care medical services, dental services, lab, radiology, pharmacy, mental health services, sports medicine, and vision services. Call to schedule an appointment.

Student Wellness and Health Promotion
G319 Student Center
(949) 824-9355, Fax: (949) 824-3919
http://www.health.uci.edu

Student Wellness and Health Promotion provides personal consults, resource information, and programming to support healthy lifestyle choices with a specific emphasis on sexual health, nutrition, fitness, substance-abuse prevention, tobacco-use prevention, and stress management. In partnership with the School of Social Ecology, the Health Center offers a survey course on health-risk lifestyle issues called Student Wellness and Health Promotion. Students interested in leadership opportunities in health can go on to become peer community health educators (a three-quarter academic course series) or earn units for volunteering in a variety of settings on campus and in the community.

Disability Services
100 Disability Services Center
Irvine, CA 92697-5250
(949) 824-7494, TDD: (949) 824-6272, Fax: (949) 824-3083
http://www.disability.uci.edu

The Disability Services Center (DSC) provides and coordinates support services and programs that enable students with disabilities to maximize their educational potential. DSC serves as a resource for the entire university community, so that students with disabilities can freely and actively participate in all facets of university life.

Lesbian, Gay, Bisexual, Transgender Resource Center
G301 Student Center
(949) 824-3277, Fax: (949) 824-3412
http://www.lgbtrc.uci.edu

The Lesbian Gay Bisexual Transgender Resource Center (LGBTRC) provides educational programs and support services to UCI students, staff, faculty, and the surrounding community.

The LGBTRC:
* Hosts programs and workshops designed to raise campus and community awareness of lesbian, gay, bisexual, transgender (LGBT) issues and heterosexism
* Provides peer counseling for LGBT issues, leadership training, volunteer opportunities, and information/referral to campus and community resources
* Provides meeting space and support for campus groups and classes
* Houses a study lounge and library of books, periodicals, and videos on LGBT topics
* Serves as a source of information and assistance to UCI's neighboring communities and as a model program for other colleges and universities

Counseling Center (Psychological)
203 Student Services I
(949) 824-6457, Fax: (949) 824-6586
http://www.counseling.uci.edu

The Counseling Center is committed to helping you achieve maximum benefit from your experience at UCI. Counseling support may include helping you to perform better academically, to cope with your emotions or to be more effective in your relationships with others. It includes helping you face academic pressures as well as pressure from family, friends and loved ones at the same time. While the counselors work with students who may be experiencing a crisis, their goal is to help you deal with your concerns before they develop into more serious problems. The services offered by the Counseling Center are designed to help you think and behave more effectively and to develop more control over your life.

Adjustment to UCI and/or the United States

Once you have settled in your new place in Irvine, you will find commonalities between where you lived before you came to Irvine and where you live now. You might find the food choices in Irvine interesting and the music familiar. You might also find you enjoy the weather. These are good indications that you are getting settled into your new environment. However, you may also experience some differences.

If you are living in another culture different from your own, there may be periods when you experience frustration, anger, alienation, depression, or other reactions that have been labeled as "culture shock." Even students who come from other states in the United States may experience culture shock. Each student reacts differently upon being in a new place with new food, music, customs, and culture.

Culture shock affects people to varying degrees and you should not feel bad, guilty, or inadequate as you adjust to your life at UCI.

Cultural Adjustment

Many experts agree that at first you may find your new situation a bit confusing. You may also find it to be exhilarating: a time of new experience, sights, sounds, and activities. The initial period of settling in often seems like an adventure with much to learn and absorb in the new culture.

During this time, you may tend to identify similarities between your home culture and US culture. You may find that people seem really friendly and helpful. You may classify aspects of the culture that seem different or even unattractive as curious, interesting, or "unusual." As you become more involved in activities and get to know the people around you, differences rather than similarities may become increasingly apparent to you. As these differences emerge, they may be troubling and sometimes shocking. Culture shock does not happen all at once. It is a feeling that grows slowly as you interact with other students, faculty, and people in the community.

Common Signs of Culture Shock

- Extreme homesickness
- Desire to avoid social settings that seem threatening or unpleasant
- Physical complaints and sleep disturbances
- Depression and feelings of helplessness
- Difficulty with coursework and concentration
- Loss of your sense of humor
- Boredom or fatigue
- Hostility towards the host country

You can try doing the following:

- Learn about and experience the new culture.
- Meet people and make new friends, both from your culture and other cultures, including those who can help you better understand and exchange cultural similarities and differences.
- Expect that there will be similarities and differences.
- Stay in contact with family and friends at home. You can call, email, FaceTime, or watch videos from your home culture.
- Talk about what you are feeling with friends who are sympathetic of your situation, or contact an advisor at the International Center. Talking about these feelings will help you overcome negative feelings about your new environment.
- Take care of yourself. Get plenty of rest, eat well, and maintain good hygiene.
- Exercise regularly. UCI's Anteater Recreation Center (ARC) offers sports, gym, exercise, and leisure activities. You do not have to pay extra to use this facility. It is already included in your tuition and fees

YOU ARE NOT IN THIS ALONE

If you are having a difficult time with your transition or adjustment to UCI, please know that there are many campus support services. Become familiar with the services, resources, and workshops offered through the Counseling Center. A great way to learn about them is to attend the weekly International hosted by the UCI Counseling Center.

The Counseling Center is the primary counseling and mental health agency for UCI students. They provide individual, couples, and group and family counseling. Contact for the Counseling Center is 203 Student Services I, 949-824-6458, http://www.counseling.uci.edu.

Ombudsman
205 MSTB
(949) 824-7256, Fax: (949) 824-2664
http://www.ombuds.uci.edu

In a system as large and complex as UCI's, you may encounter misunderstandings and disagreements and need assistance to resolve them. The UCI Ombudsman can help you, and works independently as an objective, confidential mediator. The Ombudsman has the power and the authority to ask questions of others that address and resolve a situation.

The Ombudsman:
- Listens to and discusses your questions, complaints, and concerns
- Provides answers to your questions or helps you find the person who can answer them
- Explains University policies and procedures and how they affect you
- Opens avenues of communication
- Resolves conflicts
- Mediates disputes so that an acceptable compromise for all parties can be reached
- Provides advice when a remedy is not within the jurisdiction of the Ombudsman

Police
410 E Peltason Drive, Irvine, CA 92697-4900
For emergencies, dial 911
Business Phone: (949) 824-5223 or 5224, Fax (949) 824-8567 or 0150, Lost & Found: (949) 824-1885
http://www.police.uci.edu

The UCI Police Department provides you and other members of the UCI community with public safety and police services. They are committed to respecting human dignity and to understanding the needs and values of the community. They support and assist the University of California in its mission of providing excellence in education.

Information and Technology
The Office of Information Technology, G302 UCI Student Center
(949) 824-7249, (949) 824-2222
http://www.oit.uci.edu

The Office of Information Technology (OIT) is responsible for supporting your technology needs. Having problems with your computer or printer? Don't worry. While you are fixing the problems, you can use one of the campus' drop-in computer labs. They are available in all parts of the campus.

Lab Details	Location	Hours
Gateway Study Center	Gateway Study Center (In Partnership with UCI Libraries)	UCI Libraries Gateway Study Center Hours
NS1 3116	Natural Sciences 1, 3116 (In partnership with School of Biological Sciences)	M-F: 8am - 5pm (Fall, Winter, & Spring Quarters Only)
OIT@SST	Social Science Tower 107	M-F: 8am - 9pm (Fall, Winter & Spring Quarters Only)
OIT@Student Center	Student Center C138	Student Center Hours
OIT@CCC	Cross Cultural Center 122	Cross Cultural Center Hours
SBSG 200	Social & Behavioral Sciences Gateway	M-F: 7am - 10pm, Sat: 8am - 10pm

All OIT labs require a UCInetID and Password to log in. The computers run software for writing, drawing, graphics, network communications, database management, spreadsheet and data analysis, and more. Printing is available in most labs and requires the use of a UCI Campus ID. The cost is 10 cents for black and white and 20 cents for color.

OIT also provides telephone, network, and computing services. NACS provides central computing services, computer laboratories, departmental and research-group support services, and campus-wide technical coordination. OIT provides electronic access services to all UCI students, including Educational Access (EA) e-mail accounts and access to the Internet and class information resources. Please see the EEE Web site at http://www.eee.uci.edu.

Insider Tip

Keeping track of key dates can help you save money, do well in your coursework, and graduate on time.

Selected UCI Calendar Dates

Fall 2016

September 19	Quarter begins
September 22	Instruction begins
October 7	Last day to add or drop classes without dean's approval
November 11	Holiday: Veteran's Day
November 24-25	Holiday: Thanksgiving
December 2	Instruction ends
December 3-9	Final exams
December 9	Quarter ends
December 12 -January 3	Winter break

Winter 2017

January 4	Quarter begins
January 9	Instruction begins
January 20	Last day to add or drop classes without dean's approval
January 16	Holiday: Martin Luther King, Jr. Day—no classes
February 20	President's Day
March 17	Instruction ends
March 18-24	Final examinations
March 24	Quarter ends

Spring 2017

March 29	Quarter begins
March 31	Holiday: Cesar Chavez Day
April 3	Instruction begins
April 14	Last day to add or drop classes without dean's approval
May 29	Holiday: Memorial Day
June 9	Instruction ends
June 10-15	Final exams

Important Campus Offices and Resources

Enrollment, Student Records, Grades, and Fees

Registrar Office
215 Aldrich Hall
(949) 824-6124
http://www.reg.uci.edu

The Registrar's Office maintains your student records, issues your grades, and provides you with official notifications. Below are important calendar dates that the Registrar's Office has provided. Pay attention to these dates when you make study and travel plans.

Financial Aid
102 Aldrich Hall
(949) 824-8262, Fax: (949) 824-4876
http://www.ofas.uci.edu

The Financial Aid Office can assist you with your financial needs. This office can answer questions regarding your FASFA form, student loans, scholarships, grants, and any other financial aid matters. You can also view your account and download forms through their website.

Central Cashier's Office
228 Aldrich Hall
(949) 824-6916, Fax: (949) 824-3252
http://www.fs.uci.edu/payments/general-information-about-payments/

Like most cashiers, those who work in the Central Cashier's Office work with money and do their best to make it as painless as possible when it comes time for you to give up your hard-earned dollars. They are the campus department that processes your payments for registration and other charges such as add/drops, lab receipts, readmission applications, and transcript and diploma requests. They also accept payments for bills like Student Health invoices, returned checks and library fines. They work closely with the other units in Financial Services, campus Billing Services, and Loan Services.

Campus Billing
109 Aldrich Hall
(949) UCI-BILL (824-2455), Fax: (949) 824-9807
http://www.fs.uci.edu/billing/

Campus Billing Services handles students' billing needs. If you don't receive your registration bill from the periodic campus-wide mailing, you can print a ZOT Bill fee statement which tells you the amount of your fees plus any financial aid or waivers and gives you a balance due and stub for your payment. Campus Billing Services will help you to interpret your bill, answer most of your questions, and direct you to individuals on campus who can address your concerns.

Working and Volunteering

Employment on Campus

Employment on campus is permitted for all US students. It is also permitted for all international students in valid F-1 or J-1 status. The work is limited to 20 hours per week during the quarter. Full time (anything more than 20 hours per week) is permitted during vacation periods.

For information about on-campus jobs, visit the UCI Career Center at www.career.uci.edu. You will need to have your UCI net ID activated in order to look for jobs on campus or through the UCI Career Center.

Off-Campus Employment for F1

Off-campus employment may be permitted for students who have been in valid F-1 status for at least nine months before obtaining authorization to work off-campus. Work authorization must be recommended by the International Student Advisor, and in some cases, must be approved by the US citizenship and Immigration Service (USCIS).

Off-Campus Employment for J1

Employment for J-1 students is called Academic Training. Students interested in Academic Training must schedule an appointment with an International Center advisor for information.

F-1 and J-1 students interested in working off campus must have approval before starting their work off campus.

Working off campus without authorization from the International Center or the USCIS is a violation of your student status.

UCI offers a wealth of resources to help make your time rewarding and enjoyable. Throughout your time at UCI, you'll have multiple opportunities to take advantage of them.

> *As you become familiar with UCI, you'll want to take every opportunity to make new friends, obtain new experiences, and grow as an individual. Many of the resources the campus provides will help you learn English and develop your ability to write.*

Zhang Min, a former Academic English 20D student, states,

"Don't be like me. I waited until my junior year to go to the Career Center and get a job. The best time to go to the Career Center is in your Freshman year."

Li Xiu Ying, a former Academic English 20A student, remarks,

"I loved working as a volunteer. Volunteering helped me understand Americans, improved my English, and gave me experiences I could never obtain through my studies."

Comprehension Questions

1. In what building is the Academic English Program Office?

2. Where is the Center for Excellence in Writing and Communication located? How long is an appointment with a writing specialist at the Writing Center?

3. What are three reasons to go to the International Center? Of the various services that the International Center provides, which three are the most interesting and why?

4. How can the International Peer Group (IPG) assist freshmen?

5. Where do you need to go if you are interested in worldwide opportunities to study abroad, obtain an internship, or conduct research?

6. Why does participating in the Undergraduate Research Opportunities Program help undergraduates gain valuable research experience, obtain campus recognition, and get into excellent graduate schools?

7. Why should students visit Academic Advising Offices?

8. What should students do if they find themselves on campus late at night, no other students are around, and they are afraid to walk to their residence halls alone? How can they get a free safe escort?

9. What type of services does the Student Health Center offer?

10. Where can students go to find on-campus jobs?

UCI faculty and administrators want you to graduate from UCI with the ability to communicate effectively.

66 This chapter outlines key opportunities UCI students have to obtain a wide array of resources, experiences, and information. As author Nicholas Boothman urges, "Stay open to opportunity—you never know where your next important connection will be made." 99

CHAPTER SEVEN

EXPANDING OPPORTUNITIES AND CHOICES:

Improving Your English after the Quarter has Ended

If you want to accelerate your progress learning English, you can take advantage of many opportunities and resources that are available to improve your English after the quarter has ended. Working independently on your own with some guidance during winter and summer breaks can accelerate your improvement of English.

Who might benefit from devoting time to improving English during breaks?

- All students who want to accelerate* their development of English during breaks and get a head start on the next quarter

- International students who will be returning to their home countries during breaks and are concerned about losing the English that they have just learned

- Students who have not passed one of their Academic English 20 courses and want to improve their English

*to accelerate
(verb-intransitive): to go faster than expected; if a process like language development accelerates, it goes faster than usual or sooner than you expect

> "The secret of getting ahead is getting started. The secret of getting started is breaking your complex overwhelming tasks into small manageable tasks, and starting on the first one."
>
> — Mark Twain

Academic English Bridge Activities

Below are assignments that can help you develop a plan to improve your English outside of class during breaks:

Go to a movie. Make sure to find a good one that you'll enjoy. Discuss the movie with a friend. Write a one-page analysis of the movie. Explain what you liked and did not like about the movie and why your classmates should or should not see it. Ask a proficient English speaker to read your analysis, discuss three of your strengths and three of your weaknesses as a writer, and underline your mistakes and discuss them with you. Then, rewrite your paper to correct your mistakes.

Join an online chat group or a conversation club. If possible, (consider enrolling in the Writing Center's free online conversation program offered in the summer) to practice using English.

Write a one-page reflective piece in which you consciously reflect on your language learning process (how you learn language) and improvements that you have made using English in writing.

Take one or more practice exams. They are provided in Chapter 4. Additional practice exams are posted at the Academic English Program's website. Ask a proficient English speaker to read your exam, discuss three of your strengths and three of your weaknesses as a writer, and underline your mistakes and discuss them with you. Then, rewrite your exam to correct your mistakes.

Read a magazine article and discuss the article with a friend or tutor. Here are some magazines the Academic English lecturers recommend:

- *The New Yorker*
- *The Atlantic Monthly*
- *Scientific American*
- *Time Magazine*

Write a one-page summary of an article in the magazine. Ask a proficient English speaker to read your summary, discuss three of your strengths and three of your weaknesses as a writer, underline major mistakes, and discuss them with you. Then, rewrite your summary to correct your mistakes.

Complete a number of grammar exercises from the Academic English 20 website (http://www.humanities.uci.edu/esl/). Some students say that completing ten exercises is a guaranteed way to see improvement in grammar.

Read two newspaper articles and summarize them. Each summary should be one paragraph in length. Follow the summary guidelines given in *Knowing Language*. Ask a proficient English speaker to read your summary, discuss three of your strengths and three of your weaknesses as a writer, and underline major mistakes and discuss them with you. Then, rewrite your summary to correct your mistakes.

Read a good book of your choice. Here are some books that you might read if you have not read them already:

- *Of Mice and Men*
- *Animal Farm*
- *The Old Man and the Sea*
- *Room with a View*
- *Fahrenheit 451*
- *To Kill a Mockingbird*
- *Lord of the Flies*

When choosing a book, make sure it is one you will enjoy.

– Copy ten quotations from the book that you think are important. Indicate the page number.

– Explain how each quotation adds to your understanding of the development of the plot or the characters—if you are reading fiction, and the development of the author's claim—if you are reading nonfiction.

– Ask a proficient English speaker to read your list of quotations and discuss them with you.

– Write a two-page paper, arguing why your UCI classmates should want to read the book. Ask a proficient English speaker to read your paper, discuss three of your strengths and three of your weaknesses as a writer, and underline major mistakes and discuss them with you. Then, rewrite your paper to correct your mistakes.

Improve your editing ability by doing the following on each of the above writing assignments:

- Verb Tense—Underline each verb and check its tense.

- Subject/Verb Agreement—Put an "s" above each subject and "v" above each main verb. Make sure they agree.

- Articles—Circle each singular count noun and check that it has an article or determiner.

- Word Forms—Check your dictionary to make sure all word forms are correct.

- Sentence Structure—Make sure you don't have any fragments or run-on sentences.

Improving Your Scores on Sit-Down Exams: Taking Practice Exams

Students often improve their scores on sit-down exams by taking practice exams. They say that taking practice exams builds their fluency in writing, their confidence in using English, their knowledge of vocabulary and grammar, and their ability to take sit-down writing exams.

Practice Exam: Sleep and Success

1. Put your name and the date on the front page.

2. Double-space and write about 3-3 ½ pages.

3. Read the passage below and respond to it in writing. See below for the exam question, grammar tips, and useful expressions.

Insider Tip

The Academic English Program's website can provide you access to a hyperlinked list of correction symbols and it leads you directly to helpful exercises in the specific areas you need to practice.

Key Point:

It is important that the English speaker that helps you use English well, is qualified to provide instruction, and does not simply cross out your mistakes and correct them for you. You want that person to help you identify your own errors and teach you how to correct them, so that you will gain the ability to identify and correct your own errors. Ideally, you should hire a qualified English as a Second Language writing instructor or take advantage of the free tutoring that you can obtain from the Writing Center when it is open.

4. Use a pen or pencil to write your essay. Do not take time to recopy it. Draw a line through any part of the essay that you do not want the graders to read.

5. Write as well as you can. The graders of the essay will look for grammatical correctness, organization, and comprehensibility. They will expect to see an essay that contains one clearly stated and well-supported main idea that addresses this topic and no other topic.

6. You may use an English-English book dictionary. You may not use an electronic dictionary. Your cell phone must be off.

7. Take a few minutes to plan the structure of your essay and to familiarize yourself with the "Grammar Tips and Useful Expressions."

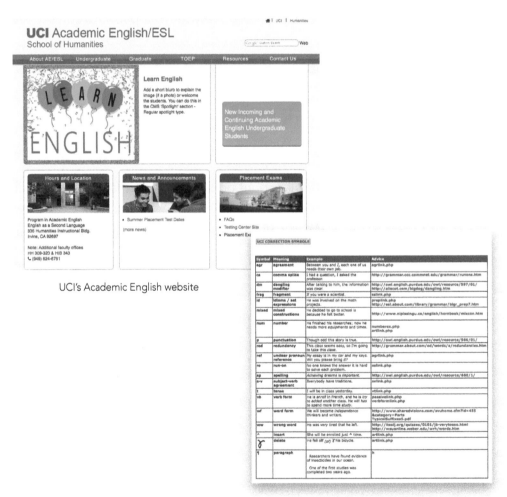

UCI's Academic English website

Program's corrective feedback symbols
http://www.humanities.uci.edu/esl/undergrad/symbols.php.

> *"It has been my observation that most people get ahead during the time that others waste."*
>
> –Henry Ford

Reading

Sleep and success are apparently woven together according to Michael Grandner, a sleep expert and researcher in neurobiology. He has found that sleep is such an important element of success in school that students who are deprived of it perform poorly on math, English, and history tests. High math scores in particular have been linked to longer sleep with fewer interruptions. Poor sleep patterns have also been linked to declining grade-point averages during the transition from high school to college. Students who go to bed at midnight or later also have rates of depression twenty-five percent higher than those who have earlier bedtimes. Unfortunately, says Grandner, young men and women between the ages of eighteen and twenty-four have the worst sleep patterns. He notes that "common knowledge is that as you get older you have more sleep problems." His research found just the opposite: Older people have fewer sleep problems than younger people.

Topic

According to Grandner, there are many disadvantages of not getting enough sleep. Do you think a healthy sleep schedule plays a role in people's success? Explain. To support your opinion, consider your own sleep habits, their possible effect on your school work at UCI, and whether UCI students are able to students maintain a healthy sleep schedule with the workload they carry.

"Learning is like rowing upstream; not to advance is to drop back."

— Chinese proverb

Grammar Tips and Useful Words and Expressions

to get a good night's sleep	Young children need to get a good night's sleep.
to be careful + to do something	We should be careful to get a good night's sleep.
to lose concentration/creativity	If we do not eat well, we can lose our creativity.
to concentrate on/focus on + something	Students need to concentrate on their studies.
to doze	I remember when I dozed off in class.
to assume that + Subject + Verb	Students sometimes assume that eating well is not important.
to restore your/our/their memories	A good night's sleep is needed to restore our memories.
to have easy/challenging/heavy workloads	Many students have challenging workloads.
to have long-term negative consequences + on something	Eating poorly has long-term, negative consequences on our health.
to believe in something	We believe in him. They believe in the value of healthy sleep patterns.
to be deprived + of something	Students are often deprived of sleep.
to be sleep deprived	I am often sleep deprived.
to need/require eight hours of sleep	I need eight hours of sleep each night.
to become susceptible to something	I became susceptible to colds when I did not take care of my health. (colds, viruses, illnesses)
to have/need an early/late bedtime	I used to have an early bedtime, but now I have a late bedtime.
to remember (v.)	I remember when we went to the museum. Generally used in the present tense when discussing past tense events when you are writing.
to have an influence + on someone	Not sleeping well had an influence on me. Going to many parties has an influence on my study habits.
to make a difference in +something	Eating healthy food made a difference in my life.
For repeated action in the past, use:	
used to + base V	I used to work at the mall, but now I don't.
would + base V	John would play tennis whenever he could.
affect (v.)	Studying affects your grades.
effect (n.)	Good nutrition has beneficial effects on health.
effective (adjective)	Studying is an effective way to raise grades

Practice Exam: Extraterrestrials

1. Put your name and the date on the front page.

2. Double-space and write about 3-3 ½ pages.

3. Read the passage below and respond to it in writing. See below for the exam question, grammar tips, and useful expressions.

4. Use a pen or pencil to write your essay. Do not take time to recopy it. Draw a line through any part of the essay that you do not want the graders to read.

5. Write as well as you can. The graders of the essay will look for grammatical correctness, organization, and comprehensibility. They will expect to see an essay that contains one clearly stated and well-supported main idea that addresses this topic and no other topic.

6. You may use an English-English book dictionary. You may not use an electronic dictionary. Your cell phone must be off.

7. Take a few minutes to plan the structure of your essay and to familiarize yourself with the "Grammar Tips and Useful Expressions."

Reading

What would you say if you met an extraterrestrial being? The SETI Institute, a non-profit organization that searches for alien life in the universe, has revealed plans to ask space enthusiasts what we should say when we meet intelligent life from other planets. So far, SETI, which stands for Search for Extraterrestrial Intelligence, has not met anyone to actually send a message to, and no one really has authority to establish diplomatic relations with an alien civilization. However, Jill Tartar, the SETI center director, wants to be ready. Some believe we should welcome new alien neighbors. Other think we should warn them to stay away. Perhaps the best approach would be to ignore them and hope they leave us alone. Tartar believes we need to be cautious because "we don't know if there are other civilizations out there, but if there are, we can be pretty sure we are the youngest." She fears earthlings might be vulnerable to more sophisticated technology that alien creatures may have, so we need to be thoughtful about how we speak to them.

– Adapted from: Johnson, John, Sr. "What Would You Say to an Extraterrestrial?" Los Angeles Times. June, 7, 2009. A9.

Topic

Write an essay in which you consider the things we should do in the event that we meet extraterrestrial beings. Should we welcome them to earth? Why or why not? What should we say? Explain why you believe your message is best.

Things to think about

If we have an encounter with extraterrestrial beings, consider whether we should we be welcoming and share earth's resources and knowledge or warn them to stay away. Should we ask them to help to solve world problems? Should we even reply?

Grammar Tips and Useful Words and Expressions

to ask noun/pronoun something	We want to ask you a question.
to send a message to noun/pronoun	We want to send a message to aliens.
to establish diplomatic relations with someone	The U.S. wants to establish diplomatic relations with China.
to ignore someone/something	We should ignore him when he shouts.
to be careful (about something)	We are careful about our homework.
to be cautious (about something)	We will be cautious about talking to aliens.
caution (n.) cautious (adj.) approach (n.)	We should take a cautious approach to aliens.
to approach (v.)	We should approach aliens with caution.
existence (n.)	Do you believe in the existence of aliens?
exist (v.)	Do aliens exist on other planets?
to be thoughtful about something	She is thoughtful about her answer.
to think about someone/something	She thinks about her reply.
should be	We should be careful about what we say.
ought to be	We ought to be cautious when we talk to them.
to believe in something	We believe in him. They believe in extraterrestrials.
to be ready + to + V	We need to be ready to go.

Vocabulary: extraterrestrial being, alien, universe, enthusiasts, intelligent life, authority, diplomatic relations, civilization, cautious, earthlings, vulnerable, sophisticated technology

Practice Exam: Fashion Trends

1. Put your name and the date on the front page.

2. Double-space and write about 3-3 ½ pages.

3. Read the passage below and respond to it in writing. See below for the exam question, grammar tips, and useful expressions.

4. Use a pen or pencil to write your essay. Do not take time to recopy it. Draw a line through any part of the essay that you do not want the graders to read.

5. Write as well as you can. The graders of the essay will look for grammatical correctness, organization, and comprehensibility. They will expect to see an essay that contains one clearly stated and well-supported main idea that addresses this topic and no other topic.

6. You may use an English-English book dictionary. You may not use an electronic dictionary. Your cell phone must be off.

7. Take a few minutes to plan the structure of your essay and to familiarize yourself with the "Grammar Tips and Useful Expressions."

Reading

In the passage below Malcolm Gladwell describes the unusual comeback of "Hush Puppies—the classic American brushed-suede shoes with the lightweight crepe sole" that had almost disappeared in early 1994.

Sales were down to 30,000 pairs a year, mostly to backwoods outlets and small-town family stores. Wolverine, the company that makes Hush Puppies, was thinking of phasing out[1] the shoes that made them famous. But then something strange happened. At a fashion shoot[2], two Hush Puppies executives—Owen Baxter and Geoffrey Lewis—ran into a stylist from New York who told them that the classic Hush Puppies had suddenly become hip in the clubs and bars of downtown Manhattan. Baxter and Lewis were confused at first. It made no sense to them that shoes that were so obviously out of fashion could make a comeback[3].

By the fall of 1995, things began to happen in a rush. First, the designer John Bartlett called. He wanted to use Hush Puppies in his spring collection. Then another Manhattan designer, Anna Sui, called, wanting shoes for her show as well. In Los Angeles, the designer Joel Fitzgerald added more space to his Hollywood store for a Hush Puppies boutique.

In 1995, the company sold 430,000 pairs of the classic Hush Puppies, and the next year it sold four times that. The year after that it sold still more. In 1996, Hush Puppies won the prize for best accessory at the Council of Fashion Designers awards dinner at Lincoln Center. (3-4)

– Adapted from: Malcolm Gladwell, *The Tipping Point*. Boston: Back Bay Books, 2002.

Topic

The unusual comeback of Hush Puppies that Malcolm Gladwell analyzes occurred before most of you were born. Think of a fashion style that became popular in your own lifetime. Explain what the fashion style was and compare the way that it became a widespread fashion trend[4] with the way that Hush Puppies suddenly became popular.

Hush Puppies store at Central Rama 9, Bangkok

---

1   *phasing out: gradually stop producing*
2   *fashion shoot: an event in which photographs are taken of people wearing fashionable clothes*
3   *comeback: to become popular again*
4   *trend: style that becomes popular*

Grammar Tips and Useful Words and Expressions

out of fashion	Those jeans have gone out of fashion.
in fashion	Something new is in fashion every season.
fashionable	She always wears fashionable clothes.
decrease/increase in popularity	That pop group has decreased in popularity.
to become popular/widespread	The new song became popular immediately.
to become a trend	The new bag became a trend on campus.
as popular as something	These jeans have become as popular as those.
more popular than something	It is much more popular than the old phone.
compared to something	Compared to your test, mine was easy.
comparable	The two situations are comparable.
similar in something	They are similar in price.
similar to something	The laptops are similar to each other.
different than	The new one was different than the old one.
unlike	This watch is unlike any others I've seen.
to be like something	This watch is just like the other one.
to differ in something	The two products differ in quality.
to be able to afford/ can afford	Most people can afford that car.
it is + (not) hard/easy for someone + to + V	It is not hard for me to understand him.
to remember (v)	I remember when we went there.
to remember + V + ing	I remember visiting them.
Generally used in the present tense when you look back as you are writing. For repeated action in the past, use:	
used to + base V	I used to work at the mall, but now I don't.
would + base V	John would play tennis whenever he could

Why don't students ask for help when they need it?

by Cindy T. Lin, UCI Extension

Often the best way to improve your English is to ask others for help. Your instructor will be happy to give you advice.

Students do not always know when to ask with for help. Below are the top reasons why students don't ask for help when they need it—before they realize that they are failing their classes.

1) "If I just keep studying or study harder, I will figure it out and do better on the next assignment."

2) "Only dumb students ask for help. Other students will think I am dumb if I ask for help. The professor will think I am dumb if I ask for help."

3) "I'll be cheating if I ask for help."

4) "I've never needed help before, so I shouldn't need it now."

5) "I need to prove that I can do this on my own."

> 66 If you want to accelerate your progress learning English and completing Academic English 20 coursework, you can take advantage of many opportunities and resources that are available to improve your English during breaks. 99

INDEX